Prepare for the Great Tribulation and the Era of Peace

Prepare for the Great Tribulation and the Era of Peace

Volume XV:
April 1, 1999 – June 30, 1999

by John Leary

Queenship

PUBLISHING COMPANY
P.O. Box 220 • Goleta, CA 93116
(800) 647-9882 • (805) 692-0043 • Fax: (805) 967-5843

Dedication

To the Most Holy Trinity

God

The Father, Son and Holy Spirit

The Source of

All

Life, Love and Wisdom

Cover art by Josyp Terelya

©1999 Queenship Publishing - All Rights Reserved

Library of Congress Number # 95-73237

Published by:
    Queenship Publishing
    P.O. Box 220
    Goleta, CA 93116
    (800) 647-9882 • (805) 692-0043 • Fax: (805) 967-5843

Printed in the United States of America

ISBN: 1-57918-122-8

Acknowledgments

It is in a spirit of deep gratitude that I would like to acknowledge first the Holy Trinity: Father, Jesus, and the Holy Spirit, the Blessed Virgin Mary and the many saints and angels who have made this book possible.

My wife, Carol, has been an invaluable partner. Her complete support of faith and prayers has allowed us to work as a team. This was especially true in the many hours of indexing and proofing of the manuscript. All of our family has been a source of care and support.

I am greatly indebted to Josyp Terelya for his very gracious offer to provide the art work for this publication. He has spent three months of work and prayer to provide us with a selection of many original pictures. He wanted very much to enhance the visions and messages with these beautiful and provocative works. You will experience some of them throughout these volumes.

A very special thank you goes to my spiritual director, Fr. Leo J. Klem, C.S.B. No matter what hour I called him, he was always there with his confident wisdom, guidance and discernment. His love, humility, deep faith and trust are a true inspiration.

My appreciation also goes to Father John V. Rosse, my good pastor who is retiring from Holy Name of Jesus Church. He has been open, loving and supportive from the very beginning.

There are many friends and relatives whose interest, love and prayerful support have been a real gift from God. Our own Wednesday, Monday and First Saturday prayer groups deserve a special thank you for their loyalty and faithfulness.

Finally, I would like to thank Bob and Claire Schaefer of Queenship Publishing for providing the opportunity to bring this message of preparation, love and warnings to you the people of God.

John Leary, Jr.

Declaration

The decree of the Congregation for the Propagation of the Faith, A.A.S.58, 1186 (approved by Pope Paul VI on October 14, 1966), states that the Nihil Obstat and Imprimatur are no longer required on publications that deal with private revelations, provided they contain nothing contrary to faith and morals.

The author wishes to manifest unconditional submission to the final and official judgement of the Magisterium of the Church.

His Holiness, Pope Urban VII states:

"In cases which concern private revelations, it is better to believe than to not believe, for if you believe, and it is proven true, you will be happy that you have believed, because our Holy Mother asked it. If you believe, and it should be proven false, you will receive all blessings as if it had been true, because you believed it to be true." (Pope Urban III, 1623-44)

The Catechism of the Catholic Church states:

Pg. 23, #67: "Throughout the ages, there has been so-called "private revelations," some of which have been recognized by the authority of the Church. They do not belong, however, to the deposit of faith. It is not their role to improve or complete Christ's definitive Revelation, but to help live more fully by it in a certain period of history. Guided by the Magisterium of the Church, the sensus fidelium knows how to discern and welcome in these revelations whatever constitutes an authentic call of Christ or His saints to the Church."

Publisher's Foreword

John has, with some exceptions, reported receiving messages twice a day since they began in July, 1993. The first of the day usually takes place during morning Mass, immediately after he receives the Eucharist. If the name of the church is not mentioned, it is a local Rochester, NY, church. When out of town, the church name is included in the text. The second occurs in the evening, either at Perpetual Adoration or at the prayer group that is held at Holy Name of Jesus Church.

Various names appear in the text. Most of the time, the names appear only once or twice. Their identity is not important to the message and their reason for being in the text is evident. First names have been used, when requested by the individual.

We are grateful to Josyp Terelya for the cover art, as well as for the art throughout the book. Josyp is a well-known visionary and also, the author of *Witness* and most recently *In the Kingdom of the Spirit*.

Early in 1999 John's bishop established a special commission to read John's published works and to talk to him about his religious experiences. The commission rendered its report in June. By letter of June 25, 1999 John was advised to have a explanatory note printed in the front of each book. This note appears on page XI of this edition.

In addition, John was instructed to have "a more learned spiritual guide advise" him before printing. This review has resulted in a priest of the Diocese of Rochester, approved by that Diocese, reading each book and delete those parts of the messages that he felt were inappropriate for any reason. As publisher we have indicated these deletions in the text with a ellipsis (...).

This first edition under these rules has resulted in a delay of 90 days. We would assume that after the next two books the delay will be less two weeks for review.

This volume covers messages from April 1, 1999 through June 30, 1999. The volumes have been coming out quarterly due to the urgency of the messages.

Volume I: July, 1993 through June, 1994.
Volume II: July, 1994 through June, 1995.
Volume III: July, 1995 through July 10, 1996.
Volume IV: July 11, 1996 through September 30, 1996.
Volume V: October 1, 1996 through December 31, 1996.
Volume VI: January 1, 1997 through March 31, 1997.
Volume VII: April 1, 1997 through June 30, 1997.
Volume VIII: July 1, 1997 through September 30, 1997.
Volume IX: October 1, 1997 through December 31, 1997.
Volume X: January 1, 1998 through March 31, 1998.
Volume XI: April 1, 1998 through June 30, 1998.
Volume XII: July 1, 1998 through September 30, 1998.
Volume XIII: October 1, 1998 through December 31, 1998.
Volume XIV: January 1, 1999 through March 31, 1999.

The Publisher

Reader's Please Note:

Bishop Matthew H. Clark, Bishop of Rochester, has accepted the unanimous judgment of a special mixed Commission set up to study the writings of John Leary. After reading the volumes and meeting with Mr. Leary, they testified that they found him psychologically sound and spiritually serious. They concluded that his locutions are not a fraud perpetrated on the Catholic community. Nevertheless, in their judgment, his locutions are of human origin, the normal workings of the mind in the process of mental prayer.

Of grave concern to the Bishop and the Commission, however, are the errors that have found their way into his writings, two of which are most serious. The first is called by the Church "millenarianism." This erroneous teaching, contained in the first 6 volumes of *Prepare for the Great Tribulation and the Era of Peace,* holds that Christ will return to reign on the earth for a thousand years at the end of time. As the *Catechism of the Catholic Church* expresses it:

> The Antichrist's deception already begins to take shape in the world every time the claim is made to realize within history that messianic hope which can only be realized beyond history through the eschatological judgment. The Church has rejected even modified forms of this falsification of the kingdom to come under the name millenarianism ..." (CCC #676).

The second error is "anti-papalism." While the Church holds that the Pope "by reason of his office as Vicar of Christ, namely, as pastor of the entire Church, has full, supreme and universal power over the whole Church" (Vatican II, Constitution on the Church, #22), Mr. Leary's locutions select Pope John Paul II to be obeyed but his successor to be ignored as an "imposter pope." This erroneous teaching is found in all the volumes.

Because Mr. Leary has reaffirmed the teaching and discipline of the Church and acknowledged the teaching authority of John Paul II and Bishop Matthew H. Clark and their successors, Bishop Clark has permitted these volumes to be published with this warning to its readers appended.

Visions and Messages
of John Leary:

Thursday, April 1, 1999: (Holy Thursday)

After Communion, I could see a large hill with a tomb on the bottom and three crosses on top of the hill. Jesus said: *"My people, I go to prepare a place for you. For it is My promise that I will welcome all who love Me into the many mansions of Heaven. In order for you to come to Heaven, as perfected souls, you must seek the forgiveness of your sins and serve your neighbor as I have shown you. As I wash your feet, I seek to wash your souls of your sins, if you would welcome Me. Cleanse your souls, My people, in the grace of My Sacrament of Reconciliation. I call you this night to pray one hour with Me in Gethsemene. Do not let sleep or your laziness get in the way of your time for prayer. You know how much prayer for peace is needed at this time in Yugoslavia. Your war plans are only accelerating you into a deeper involvement. I warned you not to start something you could not finish. Your leaders desire to continue this conflict even during these solemn feast days. Woe unto you, O men of the earth, who would rather rely on your weapons of destruction than seek a compromise of peace. Continue in your unabated prayer for peace, or your war making could involve more nations and more killing. I love you, My people. Heed My message to stopping your war before you could start a world conflagration."*

Friday, April 2, 1999: (Good Friday)

After Communion, I could see Jesus suffering on the cross. Jesus said: *"My people, it is finished. These were My Words before I gave up My Spirit. At that moment of My death, all humanity in the past, present and future were redeemed of their sins. My death was in the eternal now, so that everyone could benefit*

1

J. T.

from My gift of life. My love is so great for My people, that I was willing to die for all of you. In your earthly condition you cannot understand heavenly love. I gave you free will so you could choose to love Me by your own decision. My Gospel is a life of love that I gave all of you to imitate. When I spoke of forgiveness and loving your enemies, you could not understand how this can be. When you have faith in following My Will, anger and fighting have no place in your lives. Do not do anything to injure or kill anyone. Preserve life and make peace in everything you do. When you look at life through the eyes of faith, love of God and neighbor are all that is possible."

Saturday, April 3, 1999: (Easter Vigil)
    After Communion, I could see a lot of people in a stadium and then millions of souls in heaven. Jesus said: *"My people, Easter is a special celebration of new life in the Spirit. I suffered for a while, but then I rose triumphantly because sin and death could have no hold on Me. I came to die for all of you, but I knew that I would rise in victory. Satan thought he could conquer mankind, but he did not know the extent that I would go to grant you your salvation in My loving death on the cross. No matter what he will try, he cannot destroy My Church. That is My promise to you that I will be with you to the end of time. Rejoice in My Triumph because Satan's time is very limited. He will cause chaos in wars and contrived problems, but you will see how to endure this tribulation. Give praise and glory to God, because I am watching over you at all times."*

Sunday, April 4, 1999: (Easter Sunday)
    After Communion, I could see Jesus in His glory and in His hand was a fiery sword. Jesus said: *"My people, today commemorates My glorious Resurrection as it is a promise to My faithful, that one day they will be resurrected in their glorified bodies. While I have redeemed everyone of their sins, it is you still by your free will that must choose to love and accept Me. My sword of fire is the sword of My justice, that I will come with in judgment of mankind. I have given you the mercy of My forgiveness, but you must follow My Will and My Commandments, if you are to see eternal life with Me. I love you, My people. See that only those, who wash their robes and wear the proper wedding garments, will be the ones to enter Heaven. You have been purified and tested by your Lenten devotions. Keep true to following the*

narrow road and you will enter by the narrow gate. For those, who refuse to accept Me, are following the broad road to Hell. It is these evil ones who will taste of My fiery justice."

Monday, April 5, 1999:

After Communion, I could see a bare cross high in the sky. Jesus said: *"My people, I have risen as I have told you, but still you must follow in My footsteps. I have conquered sin and death by My dying on the cross. This was My designed means of saving all of mankind. My Resurrection was proof of My victory over Satan. I have opened the Gates of Heaven for you, but you must choose to love Me and follow My Will. I am walking with you each day to help you take up your cross to Calvary. Every one of you are presented with the cross of life. It is up to you if you will pick it up willingly and follow My Commandments. For those, who do not take up their cross, will suffer still the miseries of life in hopelessness. I offer hope to My people and I give you the gift of faith to those who believe in My Name. Easter time is a time for rejoicing in your new spiritual awakening. I offer you an opportunity to share in My love if you would only reach out and accept My love."*

Later, at Adoration, I could see large stained glass windows on many different Churches. Jesus said: *"My people, Easter is being celebrated in many churches as the ultimate in feast days. This is the time more than ever when joy should be in every heart. You are celebrating a new birth of life as My light dispels the darkness. I am the Resurrection and the Life, for without Me, you can have no life. But with Me you can share in a glorious life in Heaven. I came to give you life and real hope that you may aspire to be with Me in Heaven. Your life in this world has a certain beauty, but it will not reach its completion until you are resurrected in your glorified bodies. As you see the new signs of life in the spring, think of the greater life you can share with Me in Heaven. I invite you now, My friends, to cast aside your earthly aspirations so that you may strive for heavenly things. Do not let sin tie you down and restrain your love for Me. Seek Me as pure love and the only love that can possibly satisfy your soul. Your completeness comes closer to its perfection as you come closer to living in My Divine Will. Follow My love by pleasing Me in every way you can possibly direct your life to imitate Me. By prayer, fasting, and good works, you can strive to know Me more. You will see joy and peace come over your soul, the closer you identify with My love. See that My love is indeed the light which dispels the darkness."*

Tuesday, April 6, 1999:

After Communion, I could see all of the beautiful flowers on the Easter altar. Jesus said: *"My people, as you view these beautiful flowers around you, see them as a part of My Creation giving glory and praise to Me. These flowers are fulfilling what they were created to be by their beautiful colors and scents. You, My children, I have told you, are worth more than any of these earthly creations. For you are blessed with both spirit and body. No other creature on earth has a soul like yours. You also, were created to give glory to Me by fulfilling My plan for your life. You are a faithful witness to believe in My Name and accept My revelation that I died for you and rose on Easter morning. As you read the accounts of My appearances to My disciples in My Glorified Body, you have the proof of My victory over sin and death. It was by My Real Body that I ate the fish and allowed St. Thomas to feel the wounds of My Body. Those, who saw Me and believed, were graced in this revelation, but more blessed are those who have not seen and still believe. Faith is a gift that I freely give you and you have accepted. Continue to nourish your belief by following My Commandments and helping your neighbor in their needs. By your daily prayers and worship, you are giving glory to Me and fulfilling your purpose as My creation."*

Later, at Adoration, I could see a golden globe inserted in a table so it could be rotated and controlled. Jesus said: *"My people, I am showing you this golden globe to indicate how the men of money control your world. Through the various secret societies of world finance, you will soon see their New World Order brought about. This has been planned for many years and soon their plan for takeover will be implemented. They will soon create wars and financial upheavals that will throw the world into a panic of chaos. This will lay the foundation for the coming to power of the Anti-*

christ. As a result of a world depression and a world famine, the United Nations will call for a global government to restore order. During a time of martial law, a One World religion will be imposed which will be a means for religious persecution to force everyone to worship the Beast and take his Mark on their body. All those, who refuse this Mark, will be outlaws and liable for death.... Once the United Nations controls the world, the Antichrist will assume full control and eliminate all of the current leaders. As soon as this evil one will attain full control, I will come and sift all of these evil ones, as I will cast them into Hell in chains. My comet of chastisement will bring on My triumph over Satan, as I will then prepare the world to be renewed and made ready for My Era of Peace. Have hope, My children, for none of these evil plans will ever come to completion. I will protect My remnant with My miraculous powers, so have no fear of these evil men. They will be humbled while My faithful will be exalted."

Wednesday, April 7, 1999:

After Communion, I could see several rays of light shining down on the earth. Jesus said: *"My people, I am shining My Word of knowledge down upon you to reveal to you the meaning of My Resurrection. On the road to Emmaus I shared with My disciples many passages from Scripture of the coming Redeemer and Messiah. It was foretold that I would come from the lineage of King David and that I would suffer much to save My people. A Savior would be born of a virgin and they would look upon Him that was pierced for their offenses. I have cured the sick and the blind now can see. These were some of the signs foretold by the prophets. But the most important sign given was the Eucharist that I instituted at the Last Supper. Now, everyone can share in My Body and Blood at the breaking of the bread. The Mass is the single point that all of My believers can join and identify with My death and Resurrection. Each Mass is a renewal and fulfillment of My coming to mankind so that you could have eternal life. Each time you share in My Real Presence at the breaking of the bread, you see My graces shining into every soul at Holy Communion time. Rejoice and give thanks to God for all that I have bestowed upon you."*

Later, I could see an army person riding a multiple seated bicycle. Jesus said: *"My people, as you look on this scene involving the military and bicycles, this is an indication that soon there will be little fuel available for individuals to drive their cars. Because of the problems with your computer chips and the ongoing wars, you will see gasoline shortages to the point of rationing. As the distribution of fuel worsens by contrivance, many will have to use bicycles for transportation. This is laying the groundwork for martial law that will soon require people to take the chip in the hand to buy and sell everything. Your jobs will be next to require a chip in the hand to enter. When you see the people being forced to take the Mark of the Beast, you will know that it is time to go into hiding. Once they come to your house to force you to take this chip, those, who refuse to take it, will be imprisoned in detention centers. They will make an example out of your leaders by killing them and enslaving the rest. This test of the tribulation will be starting soon, once the Antichrist assumes power. Do not fear the Antichrist, since his reign will be brief before I will vanquish his power and cast him and his cohorts into the everlasting fires of Hell. Prepare for this time with your sacramentals and your bicycles. Refuse to take the Mark of the Beast, even if you must suffer death as a result. I will reward My faithful, but the weak, who give into the Antichrist, will suffer Hell fire as well."*

Thursday, April 8, 1999:

After Communion, I could see a shrine to Our Lady and she came in tears to say: *"My dear children, many are called to My shrines by an act of faith to follow my Call. It is not by accident that you make pilgrimages to my shrines, but a gift of grace given to you from Heaven. Many are inspired to share my messages of prayer and repentance after leaving my shrines. I am crying tears because my children are not listening to my pleas for prayers for peace in your world. You are right in asking for more prayers for peace, because there are not enough people praying to stop the world war that your world is being led to. Look at your leaders, who by their pride, are leading you deeper into war in Yugoslavia with the threat of ground troops. This has been their intention*

from the beginning. Your leaders are trying to force their will on all peoples of the world to display their power and authority. They are refusing any compromise for peace unless all of their goals are met. This attitude, for war at any cost, is from Satan, who seeks to destroy all of you by hate and pride. You are falling victim to Satan's ploys by continuing to bring war everywhere your leaders feel like it. There must be a serious effort of praying my Rosary for peace now, or you will indeed bring down a world war on yourselves. Do not be taken in by your leaders' encouragement to widen this war. Speak out and pray to stop this war or it will consume you. You cannot have peace, unless you learn love and discard this pride for power. Those, who kill their own people, will pay for their crimes. Do not forget that you are killing your own babies as well. Do not encourage more killing and destruction as a means for peace. You need to be on your knees praying my three rosaries every day, if you have hope to stop this world war and a possible nuclear attack. Pray for peace, my children, while you still have time."

Later, at the prayer group, I could see some bells tolling for the dead. Jesus said: *"My people, this bell is tolling for those being killed and those to die in the future at Kosovo. It tolls also for all of your dead babies. Be careful when you point fingers at those committing genocide, for you are killing many babies in the womb as well. Why are you afraid to think of the murdering of your babies as any less an atrocity than shooting defenseless civilians? Search for an exit to this war now before it grows wider in scope. Continue to pray for peace all over your world."*

I could see refugees being driven in trucks and buses. Jesus said: *"My people, take a look at how these refugees are being forced from their homes in Kosovo. You went through these same atrocities in Bosnia. As then and now, you are seeing your own future when such chaos will strike your land. You have been living a sheltered life without any persecution. The time of your own religious persecution will be just as ruthless by your captors. Prepare to witness a time of tribulation when you will have to trust in My help for everything you need. You are in disbelief such a thing can happen, but look back in history as you are repeating the same errors of sin."*

I could see some shrines of Our Lady as places of protection. Jesus said: *"My people, look on My mother's shrines as places of refuge. During the tribulation, these places of holy ground will be places where My angels will protect you. Your food and water will be miraculously provided there as well as many healings. When you put your full trust in Me, I will heal you in all of your spiritual and physical needs."*

I could see the roof of the ark being finished. Jesus said: *"My people, Noah was given plenty of time to build and stock the Ark, while many criticized him with jeering. As he was finishing his work, it was not long until the rains came to wipe out the evil doers of that day. I have been warning My people a long time to prepare their sacramentals, food, water, and fuel for a time of chaos when these things will be scarce. You, also, have been criticized for such preparations. But as more and more people witness the coming war clouds and the failure of your computerized devices, these people are no longer critical. Pray for those to prepare spiritually with Confession and physically with prudence."*

I could see a crucifix on a special altar in front of the Church. Jesus said: *"My people, as you witnessed My cruel Crucifixion, you can understand how ruthless man can be as the pharisees and priests were threatened by My ministry. I suffered and died on the cross for you. All I ask of you is to remember My sacrifice by keeping a crucifix on your altars. My victory over sin was accomplished through the giving up of My Body and Blood as a lamb led to the slaughter. As I brought the good thief with Me to My Kingdom, I reach out for all of you sinners to come to Me in like manner."*

I could see some mud slides and volcanoes inundate several homes. Jesus said: *"My people, because of your sins, you will suffer much before you come to your rest in Heaven. You will witness wars, and many natural disasters causing you the loss of your homes. So do not waste your precious time piling up your physical wealth. Instead, prepare yourselves with a rigorous spiritual cleansing of your faults in prayer and Confession. Follow the lives of the saints as your examples and you will have more than enough to accomplish. Show Me by your love, that you can grow close to My heart if you put your mind to achieving success in heavenly things."*

I could see much destruction and killing. Jesus said: *"My people, Satan has misled many people with killing and destroying other people's things. It is much harder to build up your society with love and care than to try and destroy it. I call on all of My children to seek peace first in their homes without divorce or abortions. You need My love and grace to follow My Will. Do not despair in thinking one person cannot overcome this evil. If each person loved their family and their neighbors, you would have no wars and killings. So focus on My love and the love of your neighbor and your society will heal itself of all of its divisions."*

Friday, April 9, 1999:

After Communion, I could see people kneeling before Jesus. Jesus said: *"My people, as My apostles looked up to Me as Lord, I am Lord of everyone's lives as well. Every knee must bend and you will bow to Me as Lord of the universe. That is why it is written that you must come through Me to get to Heaven. I will be at your judgment to declare who shall enter the Gates of Heaven. Give praise and glory to your God, who sees to all of your needs. Come to Me in adoration of My Blessed Sacrament, so you can give your allegiance to Me as the angels do every day. My Easter celebration gives you an example how you can be resurrected in your glorified bodies by following in My footsteps. All of My disciples are fishers of men and women, bringing souls to Me in conversion. Never give up hope in this world with your daily troubles, but move forward in faith to save your own souls and those you are praying for. Then on My glorious day of My Second Coming, I will greet you into My Kingdom."*

Later, at Adoration, I could see a bus and then an old black car go by slowly. The back window had been broken by stones. Jesus said: *"My people, I have given you many messages about both spiritual and physical preparation for the tribulation events, which are being witnessed all around you. The first reaction by many is that these things will not happen. They are like the foolish virgins who did not go out and buy extra oil for their lamps. I want My faithful to be like the wise virgins, who were prepared to meet the bridegroom. As you prepare spiritually, cleanse your sins at Confession and lead a prayerful life to hold fast your holiness to*

11

My Heart. Physically, set aside many sacramentals to share with your relatives and neighbors. Also, store your food, water, and fuel, always ready if you should lose your power and means to buy and sell. A time of chaos of wars and computer problems will give the One World people a window of opportunity for world takeover. Many will panic at the thoughts of no electricity and very little food. Those, who did not store their necessities, will seek to take things from those who were more prudent. When you see killing and looting for food, and the evil ones forcing the chip in the hand on everyone, you will have to go into hiding to protect your lives. You will need to keep away from the evil authorities who will seek to kill you and persecute you for believing in My Name. I will have My angels lead you away from the evil influence of the Antichrist and help you to find a safe refuge. Have no fear, but trust in My protection. This evil reign will be brief before you will enjoy My victory in My Era of Peace."

Saturday, April 10, 1999:

After Communion, I could see a light socket empty on a car. Jesus said: *"My people, when you drive your car at night and your car lights burn out, you are cast into darkness and you are afraid to go further when you cannot see. Because you want to continue driving at night, you then rush out to replace that light so you can see again. In your soul My grace is that same light of faith. While you are in the state of grace, you see clearly life's road to Heaven. When you are detoured into mortal sin, My light of grace is snuffed out and you become spiritually blind and difficult to see your way to Heaven. Why is it that you would quickly replace your lights to see physically at night, but you fail to quickly embrace My Sacrament of Reconciliation, so you can see spiritually? Do not be misled in the darkness of your sin, but search Me out in the priest at Confession, so you can renew My light in your soul. Once you have sought My forgiveness for your sins, then you can be cleansed of your sins and you will again see clearly with the eyes of faith. You can only find the heavenly road if you are full of the light of My grace. I am the Light of the world and I lead all of those who believe in My Name to eternal life. You cannot be renewed in your sinful life unless you come through*

Me. So give up your life in darkness in the love of earthly things, and exchange it for My life of love that will enlighten your soul with My Easter light."

Sunday, April 11, 1999: (Mercy Sunday)

At St. George's Church, Georgetown, Ohio, after Communion, I could see a soldier with a shield of older days. Jesus said: *"My people, I am showing you this soldier because you are all a part of this battle of good and evil. I am asking everyone, not just My apostles, to go out and preach My Gospel to all nations. Your battle is one in saving souls for Me. Satan in this age is trying to win souls for himself. Do not listen to him and show your love to Me and your neighbor. I called on My apostles and all priestly successors to forgive in My Name those sins of those who seek forgiveness. I have given you My gift of forgiveness in My Sacrament of Reconciliation. By My death, I have redeemed you from your sins. So come forward and share in the mercy of My forgiveness often. You are celebrating Mercy Sunday to make known My Divine Mercy that awaits all sinners. I seek to forgive all sinners, if you would just come to Me with a contrite heart and allow My blessing to cleanse your soul of your sins. I love you, My children, and I want you to seek perfection by living in My Divine Will. Follow Me and I will show you the road to eternal life through My love and mercy."*

Monday, April 12, 1999:

At St. George's Church, Georgetown, Ohio, after Communion, I could see some beautiful heavenly staircases that led up to heaven. Jesus said: *"My people, I have told you of the place I have prepared for you. This stairway to Heaven is a life long path that you need to follow Me and abide by My Commandments. Keep focused on this narrow road to Heaven and avoid the broad road to Hell of Satan. My love is drawing you to your Creator at all times. Do not deny Me as Judas did, but seek to be My disciples through the power of the Holy Spirit. Heaven is the goal of your soul, so learn to follow My ways instead of your earthly ways. Embrace My love with a burning desire and your souls will be graced with My abundant blessings. Whatever you seek in My*

Name, I will grant you according to My Will. I love all of you so much and I will always seek you, even in your sins. If you falter, I am here to give you a helping hand back on your road to Heaven. Have confidence and trust in Me and I will lead you to your eternal home."

Later, I could see a blurry picture of two very young girls. Jesus said: *"My people, I call you at all times to come to Me in trust like these little children. The children see the same obvious things that you do, but they come to truer conclusions because they are not as sophisticated as you adults. Many times you fail to see things in the light of faith, because you are too familiar with your daily actions. Try to look at life with a different attitude, one that is led by love and not by selfish pride. When you broaden your viewpoint to look beyond your mere wants, you will begin to see things as the innocent children, untainted by sin. It is important to cleanse your souls of your sins by going to Confession. In that way your understanding of life would not be corrupted by your sinful lives. So follow Me as children follow a parent and trust in My ways to lead you. Reach out in love to help those in need around you without being restrained by your earthly motives and comforts. It is when you go beyond simple friendship to help your neighbors, that you will see My very Self in that soul. So when you help your neighbor, you are helping Me in them. My blessings are available for all who seek them with an unconditional love. Struggle to walk with Me every day and come closer to living in My Divine Will."*

Tuesday, April 13, 1999:

After Communion, I could see some bishops wearing their miters. Jesus said: *"My people, you should be grateful for all of your priestly ministers, including the bishops, for all of their work in bringing My Sacraments to you. I am present working through My priests to bring you My graces through these sacraments. Each of My priests are blessed with a priestly vocation and are graced further with the Sacrament of Holy Orders. I continue to request your prayers for your priests and to assist them in their ministries. Your bishops have an influence on the education of these priestly vocations, so they need your prayers as well to properly instruct My priest sons. Prayers are also needed for the very vocations of priests themselves. It is important to give encouragement to those seeking the priesthood without forcing them to have certain political viewpoints. I call on My priest sons to save souls and provide Mass and My sacraments. Salvation of souls is their charge and leading prayerful and holy lives should be their example to My faithful. Satan has been attacking My priests and vocations for many years. That is why prayers of protection are needed more now than in any previous time. Make your prayers of petition for priests one of your daily responsibilities."*

Later, at Adoration, I could see a baby dressed in pink and the baby disappeared leaving the clothes behind. Jesus said: *"My people, once a baby is taken away, there is no more life as in an abortion. Each life, you snuff out, is one more life never to be loved or shared with in growing up. You have seen in wars, how children were killed by ruthless soldiers. Again, the innocents killed by Herod were based on pride of keeping his throne. But abortions involve the child's mother killing her own baby out of convenience. No reason and no price can be placed on a defense-less little one to be killed. The parents took the responsibility for this life when they conceived the child. It is not the child's fault if the parents did not want this child. I tell you that those, who kill their children, will have to answer for it at their judgment. I will forgive even this grievous sin, if the parents come to Me with contrite hearts. Those, who refuse to make amends for their crimes, will suffer much in the lowest places of Hell. For I told you how it would be better for him who harmed My little ones to be thrown into the ocean with a millstone around his neck."*

Wednesday, April 14, 1999:

After Communion, I could see flowers along the ground and an angel standing by the tomb. I asked Jesus to allow Mark, my angel, to give the message. Mark said: *"I am Mark, who stands before your God. The women at the tomb were greeted by an angel who stated: 'Why seek the living among the dead? He is risen.' This was the first heralding of Jesus' Resurrection to the women at the tomb. Many of the disciples did not understand the words of Jesus when He said He would rise in three days. The glorious words, 'He is Risen.' gives testimony to those seeking Jesus' body that He is alive and among the living. The Resurrection of Jesus was proven to His disciples by His appearances to them. These accounts in Scripture are your proof of the glory of God that He offers to each soul. The example of Jesus rising from the dead is a hope for each believer that one day they will be resurrected as well. Then all of those faithful to Jesus will also be among the living in Heaven, instead of the dead in Hell. Rejoice, my children, you should have joy in your hearts every day for all that the Lord has given you. Give praise and glory to Jesus for His victory over sin."*

Later, at Adoration, I could see some homeless refugees struggling to survive. Jesus said: *"My people, have pity on those less fortunate with your time and your money. You need to take a responsibility in helping the needs of your neighbor. Every time you reach out to help someone, you are helping to ease the pain of My Mystical Body. No matter how poor a person's circumstances are, they still have My presence in their soul. You see My reflection in their eyes of hope. Lift them up in your support and help dispel their despair by sharing your love with them. If not for some circumstances, you could be in their place. I love all of My children and these downtrodden no less than those better off. Those, who have been given many blessings, need to share their excess with those who have little. When I was on the cross, My people treated Me as a lowly criminal. I know all the sufferings and frustrations of man, but My Resurrection gives everyone a new hope in the Spirit of My life. Do not despair with life's troubles, but look forward to the day of your own resurrection. After this life of tears, My faithful can look ahead to the joy of Heaven above and heaven on earth in My Era of Peace."*

Thursday, April 15, 1999:

After Communion, I could see people in the pews at Mass. Jesus said: *"My people, you will be tested much in this life, especially during the time of tribulation. You will endure many sufferings as I did in life, but I will not disappoint you in helping your drooping spirit. No matter how hard your struggles in life may be, always seek My help and I will bring rest to your soul. You will find peace in prayer and receiving Me in Holy Communion. Without these little respites, life would be much more difficult. So reach out to Me in faith and hope, and you will be able to cope with all that you will face in life. Working each day for your keep is not unusual, even I worked with My foster father to ply a trade. The work of your hands is a proper means for your salvation. You employers should not abuse your employees and pay them a proper wage. The employees also, should give a fair day's work for their pay as well. When all of you are in harmony with My love for each other, your labor is one of love. Be secure in your lives that I will be watching over each of My children."*

Later, at the prayer group, I could see Mary praying at the tomb and Jesus above her in His glorified body. Jesus said: *"My people, I appeared to the women at the tomb and then later to My disciples. In My appearances I gave hope to My followers amidst the sorrow of My loss. I explained to them how I had to die to redeem all of mankind from their sins. Every time you celebrate My Resurrection, I lift up the souls of My faithful out of their darkness and into My light."*

I could see a cornerstone of a building. Jesus said: *"My people, many times I gave parables to the Scribes and Pharisees speaking how My Church was being taken away from them and given to My disciples. It was for these threats to their position that they killed Me on Calvary. So I am indeed the cornerstone that was rejected. Now with My victory over death and sin, the Gates of Hell will not prevail over My Church, as it will last to the end of time. Time will pass away, but My Words will not pass away."*

I could see some ladders with flames to the side. Jesus said: *"My people, these fires represent the many evil influences which you have to struggle through. I come to give you ladders to escape your sins and I put out the fires of the evil ones with My peace and love. Struggle every day to do My Will in obeying My Commandments. Those, who follow Me in faith, have nothing to fear. I will bring My faithful to their heavenly reward, while the evil ones will face eternal hell fire."*

I could see an old Church as the front door was being closed. Jesus said: *"My people, why have you disfigured My churches by stripping them of all that is reverent and holy? Because you have abused My places of worship, you will soon see these churches taken away from you in a religious persecution. Prepare for the day when you will only have your Rosary as the tribulation proceeds."*

I could see a yellow life raft being thrown into the water to save some people in the water. Jesus said: *"My people, you have drifted away from Me in your wars and your sins. No matter how much you have offended Me, I still give you My life raft of Confession to save you from your sins. Those, who have sorrow in their hearts and seek My forgiveness of their sins, will be led to a new life of love in the Spirit. Be thankful for My graces which I make available for you to cleanse your sins."*

I could see some blessed candles. Jesus said: *"My people, I call on you to store up your sacramentals since soon they will be hard to replace. Your blessed candles would be most useful at underground Masses as well as giving light during the three days of darkness. In many miraculous ways I will protect My faithful in ways you cannot imagine. My Church will survive even the tribulation and all the evil spirits in their actions."*

I could see St. John and St. Peter being whipped for their faith. Jesus said: *"My people, it is one thing to say you believe in My Name. It is another to be willing to suffer persecution for that belief. My apostles, once strengthened with the Holy Spirit, were defiant of being persecuted for believing in My Name. They actually were grateful that they could witness to Me by being whipped. You, too, My faithful, must call on the power of the Holy Spirit to proclaim your faith in face of persecution. Many are risking prison and beatings to protect the unborn. This is the same spirit of defiance that My disciples demonstrated. Are you willing to suffer for your belief in My Name? You will be tested further in refusing to take the Mark of the Beast for buying and selling. I tell you again to give up your life for Me than worship the Antichrist and take his Mark. Those, who take this Mark knowingly, will suffer a living Hell on earth and below. Give praise and glory to Me if you should be called to suffer and even risk your life for My Name. I will be at your side to protect your soul and ease your pain."*

Friday, April 16, 1999:

After Communion, I could see a tear in some clothing. Jesus said: *"My people, when you have a sufficient tear in some clothing, no amount of mending can fix it. It is better to start making a new piece of clothing. So it is with your spiritual lives. When you are leading sinful lives, it is not enough to say you are going to change. You need to call on My help in Confession and start over with a completely different view. I came to fulfill the law, but with a whole new view through the love of God and neighbor. Man's ways are imperfect and in need of My love. When you follow My ways of love, they will lead you on your road to perfection. Your fighting and complaining are all based on selfish and uncompromising motives. I call on you to love and forgive your enemies and to go the extra mile in helping your neighbor. I call on you to come out of your comfort zone to help others and share from your bounty of My blessings."*

Saturday, April 17, 1999:

At St. Cecilia's Church, Rockaway, N.J., after Communion, I could see God the Father symbolized in the burning bush that was not consumed. God the Father said: *"My dear people, you have just celebrated again My Son's Resurrection. Jesus is the gift I have given you so the sins of all mankind could be atoned for. I have sent My only begotten Son so that you may have life in the Spirit. Since the time of Adam's sin and the Gates of Heaven were closed, I promised My people that I would send a Redeemer, the Messiah to come. Jesus has come to you and He died for all of you on the cross. That is why this Easter celebration is so glorious, because you have been redeemed and the Gates of Heaven have been opened up to you. In order to be judged worthy of Heaven, you must accept My Son as your Savior, seek the forgiveness of your sins and obey My Commandments. I want to thank you again for the dedication of your prayer group and your prayers in honoring Me this year. Even more, I want to thank those working to bring about your conference in My honor. I bless all of those who call on Me in prayer and I will bless your work on heavenly things as well."*

Sunday, April 18, 1999:

At St. Cecilia's Church, Rockaway, N.J., after Communion, I could see an altar, but the curtain behind it had chips spaced out on it. A person was wearing a chip on a watchband. Jesus said: *"My people, a time is coming soon when you will be worshiping your technology instead of Me in your churches. You will see images of the Beast on your altars, as the Antichrist will attempt to force people to worship him as their god. Do not listen to anyone who claims to be Me. Do not take his Mark on your hand or forehead for your jobs or food. I will have My angels provide for you in your needs. Have faith and trust in Me and your souls will be protected. Even if they threaten you with death, never give in to the Antichrist and his agents. Those, who knowingly take the Mark of the Beast and worship him, will suffer hell on earth and below."*

Later, at Blessed Virgin Mary of Help, Queens, New York, I could see a large Host being raised. Jesus said: *"My people, as My disciples recognized Me at the breaking of the bread, I want you to recognize My Real Presence in the Consecrated Host and Wine. You see the bread and wine, but with your eyes of faith, you see My Body and Blood. The Mass is the most important prayer for you, because you see the miracle of My Transubstantiation at every offering of the Mass. I love you so much that I continue to share My Body and Blood with you at every Eucharist. I gave My life up so you could have life in My Spirit. It is through My Mystical Body that you help Me in your neighbor. So come to Me in love and receive My Real Presence. Give Me thanks at Communion and your visits of adoration before My Host. I ask you to manifest your love for Me by obeying My Commandments. I treasure the time you take in adoring Me and your moments with Me after Holy Communion. Your soul is seeking Me to be satisfied by giving Me praise and glory."*

Monday, April 19, 1999:

At St. Cecilia's Church, Rockaway, N.J., after Communion, I could see some doors open. Jesus said: *"My people, when you have visitors to your house, you clean your house and make them comfortable in their stay. It may involve making some bedding accommodations and feeding them meals. It is similar when you welcome Me when I knock on the door of your heart. In preparation for My entrance, you need to tidy up your soul by going to Confession. I am in search of you purifying your souls of your sins and changing your lives. For one, who does welcome Me, I will share My graces and love with that soul. Your decision to*

love Me will allow My rest to enter your soul and you will experi-
ence My peace. For those, who do not answer My call, because
they have no time for Me, they will be always searching for peace,
but they will not find it. I will continue to pursue each soul in
love, but I cannot share with you unless you open the door to
your heart. Do not be ashamed to let Me enter and see your sin-
ful heart, but be open to make amends with a contrite heart."

Tuesday, April 20, 1999:

At Church of the Assumption, Coldsville, Pa., after Communion, I could see a song book in a balcony for a choir. Then I saw a
road with exquisite silver crosses in a line along the road. Jesus
said: *"My people, you have heard the reading of how St. Stephen*
was stoned to death. Whenever a soul is martyred for My Name's
sake, all of the angels in Heaven are singing for the glory of God
in this new martyr. They greet this soul with instant sainthood
for being faithful. In the vision you are seeing these exquisite
crosses, because it indicates the beautiful entrance into Heaven
for each martyr. So do not be fearful of these evil men and evil
spirits. Pray for My help and I will protect your souls through all
of the tribulation. Even if you should be martyred, I will comfort
your pain so you will not be tested beyond your endurance. Your
time here on earth is very short. So do not be concerned to live a
long life. It is your eternal destiny that is the most important. By
a prayerful life and devotion to following My Will, you will be
guided to Heaven. Ask for My grace and I will bring you to your
glorious place in Heaven."

Later, at a private chapel before the Blessed Sacrament in Pennsylvania, I could see a rock removed from an opening in a stairway, as the Antichrist walked up the stairs. Jesus said: *"My people,*
the time is ripe for the Antichrist to soon make his presence known.
Once exposed, he will quickly ascend to power over all of the
earthly leaders. He will take control of the United Nations and be
the head of the One World religion. Once in control, he will do
away with all of the world's leaders, so he can have full control.
As head of the One World religion, he will attempt to force every-
one to take the Mark of the Beast and have everyone worship him
as a god. He will claim to be greater than Me and all of the proph-

ets. He will manifest miracles of demonic power. Beware when the Antichrist will come to power, so that you will not be under his influence. Flee from your cities and never take or worship the Mark of the Beast. Have no fear, My faithful, for as the Antichrist assumes full power, I will crush him. By My triumphant chastisement, I will cast him and all the evil people and evil spirits into Hell, where they will be chained. I will then raise up My faithful remnant and re-create the world again with no evil in My sight. You will then enjoy My Era of Peace on earth. Rejoice in My glory and be ever thankful for My saving your souls."

Wednesday, April 21, 1999:

At a private chapel in Pennsylvania after Communion, I could see an eagle and it was locked in chucks as a prisoner. Jesus said: *"My people, as I told St. Peter, another will take you by the hand and restrain you in chains. You will be held against your will for the sake of My Name. I tell you, people of America, you are the eagle of this vision that will be held fast as well like prisoners. As Israel was a captive nation during the Babylonian Exile, you also will be a captive nation in payment for all of your sins and your unforgiving spirit in the face of My justice. My mercy is upon those who seek to have their sins forgiven, but My wrath of judgment will fall on those who reject Me. I have given many warnings to prepare your souls for the events of these last days. Soon you will see your captivity come about as the agents of the Antichrist will carry out their plans for your capture. For those, who are in hiding, My angels will watch over you and provide for your needs. For those in captivity, you may suffer martyrdom, torture or enslavement. Pray that through this tribulation, you will be faithful to My love. It is by My grace of protection that you will be saved. Rejoice as these events come to pass, since My victory over Satan will swiftly cast him and his cohorts into Hell in their own chains. My faithful will then witness to My glory on earth and in Heaven."*

Later, at Adoration, I could see a monstrance for adoration with the Host. Jesus said: *"My adorers of My Blessed Sacrament, I want to thank all of you for taking time to visit Me. Many come to give adoration and praise at their appointed times and they are faithful to their hours. I give each soul a special blessing for their intentions of praise. You have honored Me here on earth, but when you come to the Gates of Heaven, I will honor you before My Father, and allow you to enter. Those, who pray to Me and visit My Blessed Sacrament, know My voice and I recognize them as well. But those, who do not pray and do not seek forgiveness, I will say to them, 'Out of My sight, you accursed, because I know you not.' Continue to adore Me while you still have time. A day will be coming when the Antichrist will use My places of adoration for abominations of evil sacrifice. So, enjoy your places of peace in My Real Presence, while you still have Me before you."*

Thursday, April 22, 1999:

After Communion, I could see a bee up close with nectar as it was flying from flower to flower. Jesus said: *"My people, you see the bees going about their daily tasks of bringing nectar back to their colonies for their food. They share their food in common as they fertilize the flowers and fruit trees. You all have similar tasks as you go through your days. You go to work so you can provide the food for your families. But when you come to share in My Eucharist of the Mass, you are sharing My Heavenly Bread in common among all of My Mystical Body. I am the Bread of Life by which all of you are fed spiritually with the graces of My Sacrament in Holy Communion. As you go out into the world, you are to fertilize other souls with the knowledge of My saving power. Give example in living holy lives to show your love for Me and your neighbor. Bring as many souls to Me as you can, so they can recognize My Real Presence in the breaking of the bread. Bread is crucial food in your physical diet. My Heavenly Eucharist is the spiritual bread which is the food of the soul, that keeps you fully nourished in My peace and love. Without coming to Me, you will die of a spiritual famine. So come to your Lord and Master so you may have life in the Spirit."*

Later, at the prayer group, I could see a spark plug with a red glow around it. Jesus said: *"My people, this vision indicates that you are only a spark away from a much wider conflict. As each day goes by, plans are being made to escalate the war instead of reaching a compromise. Saving face to stop this conflict shows*

Josyp Terelya
1998

To ronto

that pride is involved on both sides. Satan will use all means to ignite this war into a world war. My prayer warriors must step up their efforts in praying for peace. Pray harder while you can still mitigate the extent of this war."

I could see a dark cloud and a tornado coming down. Jesus said: *"My people, there are dark clouds of judgment lying over your country. As people protest your abortions, others are warping the laws to their own end of persecuting these protesters. Money and a false sense of rights to kill are all a part of your*

death culture. Your killing of My babies has brought many chas-
tisements on your possessions. Life is more important than things
or conveniences. Treasure the value of life more than your
earthly comforts."

I could see a crowd of children trying to get out of a school.
Jesus said: *"My people, this latest trial of killings is a further*
example of the effects of your death culture on young adults.
Many parents are not even aware of the effects of your evil TV
programming and virtual reality computer games that are brain-
washing your children with evil. Your computer networks are now
providing ways for children to make bombs and secure weapons.
Your permissive society of seeking instant gratification has raised
your movies and programs to a violence level that makes this
latest carnage into a reality. Seek to bring My love into your fami-
lies before Satan destroys you."

I could see many infants sleeping on blankets. Jesus said: *"My*
people, bringing children up in your evil environment is becom-
ing a challenge for any parent. These new parents desire safe
streets and a safe school, but this is harder to find. Why are people
intent on killing and exploiting children for sex and drugs? Money
is at the root of many of your vices. Evil people behind the scenes
continue to support a drug culture and an abortion mentality
mostly for money. Until you cleanse your cities and towns of this
evil lot, your problems will only worsen."

I could see a large picture of Lenin and symbols of communism. Jesus said: *"My people, plans for undermining your coun-*
try by attacking the family has been a goal of the communists
from the beginning. A sense of victory over atheistic communism
has only been a facade to hide their real intentions of destroying
your country. Love of God and love of neighbor has been turned
into love of self and love of things by your advertisers. What is
being taught in your schools is the reason why your country is in
decadence and headed for ruin. You are reaping the harvest of
your sins and the wages of sin brings death to the spirit. Wake up
to all of your evil ways before they consume you."

I could see some dead bodies in the streets. Jesus said: *"My*
people, your news reports daily killings, while your violent TV
programming shows everyone how to kill. Is it any wonder that

your children are imitating what they see? The real problem of your society starts with the evil influence of violent programs, even in your cartoons. Why are you aghast at these latest killings when children can watch this every day? Wake up, America, and get rid of your violent programs and movies. It would be better to turn off your TVs and stop going to movies until movie makers clean up their acts. Get rid of your drugs and pornography and your children will have a better environment for proper living."

I could see some garbage cans being stuffed with trash. Jesus said: *"My people, as you are bent on spring cleaning, carry this over to your spiritual cleaning. Many of your children are lacking love because you do not give them enough loving attention. Put aside all of your selfish interests and extra jobs so your children can have a loving family environment. When you have little contact with your children, you are breeding ways they will struggle to get your attention. Prayer in the family is also important to hold your family together in love. Without My presence among you, Satan will be causing more divorce and killings. Unless you can establish peace and love in your own families, you will not have peace in your world. Pray for each other that peace will be brought to families, nations, and the world."*

Friday, April 23, 1999:

After Communion, I could see a white misty light in a cave. There was a huge pile of canned food that came miraculously, not in a planned storage. Jesus said: *"My people, many have difficulty in placing their full trust in My providing you with food during the tribulation. My angels will lead you to caves of protection. Do not take food or the Mark of the Beast from the Antichrist and his agents. I will provide you food miraculously as I did for the people in the Exodus. When you give your will to follow Me, I will reward your faith in ways you do not understand. You will need My angels to protect you from the demons and for bringing you My Heavenly Manna in spiritual Communion. Do not fear this time, for My help will be with you when you ask Me in prayer. Have trust in Me during the coming tribulation and I will provide you protection, food, and water. Be prepared in prayer with your sacramentals."*

Later, I could see a gleaming brass device hanging from the ceiling. Then I saw some cameras in various places. Jesus said: *"My people, as your technology has improved, you are now being watched by security devices wherever you go. Many of these chips can scan without usual cameras, so you do not even know you are being watched. The one world people want to know and control all of your movements. That is why your governments are using so many cameras and satellites to watch you. Soon your travel will be more restricted and it will be more difficult to travel over national borders. Even your expressways will soon require smart cards to travel them. As the Antichrist gains in power, he will promote the Mark of the Beast for travel, food, and jobs. Everything will soon have to be purchased and sold using smart cards and eventually with chips in the hand. Go into hiding before they try to force the chip on you. Call on My help and My angels will protect you even through the tribulation. Have patience but a brief time before I will cleanse all the evil off the earth. You will then be rewarded with My Era of Peace."*

Saturday, April 24, 1999:

After Communion, I could see a night scene and someone driving to avoid some pot holes. Jesus said: *"My people, when you are driving around pot holes, it is not easy to avoid all of them, especially in the dark of night. Life's troubles are like this as well. You do everything practically to avoid trouble, but sometimes you run into difficulties you cannot avoid. These are the times that you must call on My help when you remember to do so. Your troubles are going to only worsen as you draw closer to the tribulation of the Antichrist. In these coming difficulties, they will be beyond your physical handling of them. It is for this reason that I have been giving you warnings of how to prepare both spiritually and physically. You will not be tested beyond your endurance, but you must turn to My help so I can bring you miraculous protection and provide for your needs. The readings speak of the disciples believing that they must eat My Body and drink My Blood to be saved. Indeed, you can only have eternal life through Me. There is no other choice. Satan will sift those who do not seek My help and they will be lost. So trust in*

My help and believe that I am your only Savior, and you will save your souls."

Later, I could see someone carrying a cross in the sands of the seashore. Jesus said: *"My people, for many years My faithful have taken up their crosses. That is why this vision of a seashore represents the sands of time. I call on you to make sacrifices and make visits before My Blessed Sacrament. Those, who suffer a cross for Me, will have many rewards of My graces. Your life is that opportunity to reach out and save souls for Me. So continue to struggle on carrying your own cross every day, knowing that each day you suffer, it draws you one day closer to being with Me in Heaven. You will fall and stumble many times, but pick yourself up and be persistent in your belief in Me. Follow in My footsteps and the footsteps of those in history who believed in My Word and carried it out in their daily lives."*

Sunday, April 25, 1999:

After Communion, I could see Jesus sitting on the throne of heaven and there were angels along both sides leading to Jesus. Jesus said: *"My people, I am showing you how you will be greeted in Heaven for all of those who accept Me into their hearts. All Heaven rejoices as each saint is welcomed into Heaven. Enter the narrow Gate to Heaven, which means you have to be purified to reach perfection before you can enter. I am the Good Shepherd who calls My sheep home. I am the sheepgate through which every soul must come to receive eternal life in Heaven. My sheep hear My voice of love and they must decide with their free will to accept Me in both word and deed. Satan offers you only hate and empty promises, because he despises you. Seek My love and mercy and your soul will be fully satisfied. Do not listen to the evil one and the lure of only earthly things and pleasures. Search for a higher life by following My Will in My plan for your life."*

Monday, April 26, 1999:

After Communion, I could see a wave of tongues of fire come over the people. Jesus said: *"My people, as St. Peter witnessed the blessing of the Holy Spirit on the new converts, you also are receiving the Holy Spirit in Baptism and Confirmation. Every time that you share in one of My seven sacraments, you are embracing the gifts of the Holy Spirit. As you come to Mass and receive Holy Communion worthily, you are receiving Me in the Eucharist and the Trinity as well. When you receive one of the Persons of the Trinity, you receive all three Persons, because We are inseparable. That is why you should use the gifts of the Holy Spirit that are available to you in order to spread My Gospel message. As you delight in the spirit of the Easter season, you should share your joy in faith with all of those around you. Life is too short to not share your love with your neighbors. Let the fire of the Holy Spirit in you empower you to evangelize where you can witness your love to others."*

Later, at Adoration, I could see unborn babies being placed in a garbage can. Jesus said: *"My people, how can you not see the ongoing holocaust in your own hospitals? These precious little lives are being snuffed out before they could even be born. Are you not ashamed of all of this killing going on in your own country? The doctors performing your abortions know fully well that they are killing babies, and they will be held responsible for the taking of these lives. When they clean the womb, they have to account for all of the body parts, so none are left behind. These babies are no less human at any stage from conception. The mothers, who allow their babies to be killed, are responsible as well for these deaths, no matter how much they want to rationalize they are not human. Those, who stand by and watch this killing going on, are also responsible for allowing this to take place. My faithful need to be praying for abortions to stop, but you must be working actively to discourage this killing. You can work to change your evil abortion laws or educate the mothers of the preciousness of life. You are quick to protest the atrocities in Kosovo or the killings in Littleton, Colorado, but why are you not protesting the millions of My babies being killed each year? Life is precious in all of its stages. If you cannot impress your children with the value of life, then how will you stop them from killing others in the future?*

Tuesday, April 27, 1999:

After Communion, I could see twisted strands of DNA symbolizing life's blueprint. Jesus said: *"My people, in your quest*

for knowledge, your scientists have discovered the workings of the genes in a cell's DNA. But man was not satisfied with knowing how life works. Now you are trying to improve on My plans of creation. All of your efforts to improve a plant or a person's DNA will end in ultimate failure, because you lack the total understanding of My plan for life. Man is always trying to exploit nature for profit, but you ultimately end up losing your goal. Your failures in creating antibiotics that will kill all diseases, have created monster mutants of diseases with no cures. Whenever you try to manipulate My plans for life, you will continue to meet failure. Instead of working against My plans, you should be following My Will to lead you both in physical and spiritual ways. My ways are better than your ways. It is your pride and stubbornness that bring you in conflict with My plans. This is why I have given you My Commandments to guide you on your path through life. When you conform in love of God and neighbor, you will see harmony in both your physical and spiritual lives."

Later, at Adoration, I could see a large Host with a large blue mantle all around the Host. Jesus said: *"My people, My mother brings many souls to Me through her signs and the Rosary. Look on My Host as your bread of life. As the tribulation is coming, you must prepare for this spiritual battle between good and evil. Your breastplate will be your faith and your helmet will be your right reason formed by a proper conscience. You must build up your strength by wearing your blessed sacramentals, saying your daily prayers, and receiving Me worthily in daily Communion. I bestow My abundant graces on those following My Will and on those who receive My Sacraments. It is these graces of protection and the protection of your guardian angels that will sustain you during the tribulation. When the Antichrist assumes power and the demons are released from Hell, man will be tested by an evil you have yet to experience. Have no fear, since My power is greater than Satan and all of his demons. Pray and trust in Me and I will bring you safely through this trial so you may enjoy My Era of Peace on earth."*

Wednesday, April 28, 1999:

After Communion, I could see a dark door leading to a crypt underneath the Church. Jesus said: *"My people, as you read about My early Church, I want you to remember the fervor of the spirit of faith. It is this same persistence in believing in My Word that will lead My underground Church during the coming schism.... I have told you that the Gates of Hell will not prevail over My Church. You have My assurance that My remnant will remain faithful to My Word. You will have to go underground, because the public churches will be joined under a One World religion that will be faithful only to the Antichrist.... You will be fortunate to have a priest for an underground Mass. Fear not during this time for you will know My victory will be close at hand. If you cannot find a Mass, you can call on Me in spiritual communion and I will have your guardian angel deliver My Heavenly Host on your tongue. I will perform miracles of protection and provide for your needs. Have faith in Me and I will protect your souls from the evil ones."*

Later, at Adoration, I could see some virulent germs under the microscope. Jesus said: *"My people, you need to know that Satan is behind all of the efforts for zero population growth, because he wants to destroy man. He tries to influence women to kill their babies in the name of women's rights and convenience. Satan has lulled many to believe that babies are only fetuses or anything but human. In euthanasia people are convinced to kill to stop pain or seek only a quality of life. The truth of killing in abortion and euthanasia is never admitted by those making money on this carnage. Satan is also encouraging nations and ethnic groups to fight for land. Again money is made in weapons as more lives are taken in these wars. Some evil men are also working on biological warfare which can kill many innocent people through designed viruses. Even Satan worship, evil movies, and evil computer games are influencing your children to kill each other. Once you realize that you are in a battle between good and evil, you can see how all of the evil forces are seeking to destroy man. Come to Me, My faithful, with prayer and fasting to fight this spiritual battle which has created your death culture. I am the Resurrection and the Life of the soul. Those, who follow Me, will be saved. Satan is an angel of lies and death. Those, who serve him, will be lost in eternal hell fire. Choose to follow Me, and My love will surround you. Choose Satan and only hate and misery will be your future."*

Thursday, April 29, 1999:

After Communion, I could see a very ordinary painting on the wall with a light shining from it. Jesus said: *"My people, you must have discernment of the End Times that you are in and not always seeking signs. The only sign I gave to My people was the sign of Jonah. My Scriptures give you signs of the End Days, but do not worry since these things will happen in My time and according to My Will. You have seen various miracles as well, but I only healed those who had faith and believed in My power. The miracles, you should seek, are the changing of hearts through My helping your evangelization efforts. When souls renounce their earthly ways and seek the forgiveness of their sins in Confession, all Heaven rejoices over the saving of one soul. Seek to spread the love of God and love of neighbor through My Gospel. This is why I told My apostles to teach all nations about Me. It is the same desire I have for all of My faithful that they love one another. You may be given miracles of My grace in some signs, but look to the fruit of every work in how it brings souls to conversion."*

Later, at the prayer group, I could see an unusual amount of insects and grasshoppers eating up some crops. Jesus said: *"My people, your drought and bad weather will continue to worsen until your crops will be endangered. You will see a chastisement of insects that will attack your fragile crops. Pray, My children, that you will find enough to eat during a coming world famine. I have asked you to store one year's supply of food and water for when it will be scarce. Pray that enough people will heed My words of warning. I will multiply what you have, if you would just have faith in My Word."*

I could see large groups of protesters in the streets in many cities around the world. Jesus said: *"My people, many will be protesting the atrocities of many injustices. People will be frustrated with low paying jobs and various shortages of your necessities. These problems will worsen at the end of the year and it may trigger the instability of many governments and financial systems. Be prepared to endure major chaos right before the Antichrist will take over."*

I could see some pictures and statues of older leaders. Jesus said: *"My people, in days of the past your leaders had more in-*

tegrity and feeling for the people. Today, I am missing in many of your lives because you only give Me lip service. The hearts of today's leaders are very ruthless and calculating for power and control of money and people. Your leaders are becoming more like dictators than statesmen. Your society has bred such leaders because they are a mirror image of your sins and your lack of belief in My Gospel. Pray for your leaders, both the secular and the religious."

I could see long lines of people, thankful to receive some soup from some large kettles. Jesus said: *"My people, you have seen soup lines with the refugees and also in your cities for the homeless and destitute. Have mercy on these people and help them with your charity. A time is coming when you may be in such lines at the prison camps. As you see religious persecution increase, many of your possessions will be stripped from you. Your rights to freedom will soon come to an end under martial law. Do not be shocked that this will happen in your country. You already are close to a police state to keep order. Pray for peace among your neighbors before they try and kill you for the spoils of your possessions."*

I could see some violent words of graffiti on some wooden walls. Jesus said: *"My people, your death culture is breeding hatred and discontent among various classes of people. The poor will become more demanding of their share of your current prosperity. Only the rich and well to do are profiting from your mergers. Many are facing unemployment or low paying jobs as a result. There are many signs of this increasing violence and frustration even among your schools. These evils are increasing because you do not trust in My help, but trust only in your own means. Without following My ways, you will see your country quickly fall into ruin. Your society is declining from within as the Roman empire did. Change your ways before it is too late."*

I could see some soldiers and many were fearful of them in their own town. Jesus said: *"My people, a day is coming when your own military will be used against you to hold you in detention centers that look like prison camps. By your disrespect for life, life will not be cherished as it should. Evil men will purge those they dislike for any reason. When you are faced with the coming police state, your rights will be non-existent and you will be hiding from the authorities. Pray for strength when you will be tried during this evil battle."*

I could see a woman of saintly stature working to bring the pope to Rome. Jesus said: *"My people, the saint of today is St. Catherine of Siena. She lived in the time of several Antipopes when three popes claimed the throne of St. Peter. You are soon to see a time of schism in My Church once again.... Be strong in your faith, because you will be tested even with martyrdom for your beliefs. I will be helping you in miraculous ways. Do not be afraid to witness to your faith, because many will criticize you as they did Me."*

Friday, April 30, 1999:

After Communion, I could see a light reflect off a floor that led to an altar in a Church. Jesus said: *"My people, I am the truth and the life, and the truth will set you free. My light leads you down the path of life. I am guiding you at your side every day as I show you the road to Heaven. It is not impossible to be a saint and enter Heaven. Your life is one long opportunity to grow in your faith and learn to follow My Will. There will be times that your earthly life may cloud your heavenly goal, but when you keep focused on Me in Confession, I can forgive your sins. If you imitate My life by following My Gospel, you will see your way back to My ways. Many of your failures come from following your own imperfect ways, rather than My ways. Through daily prayer, the sacraments and occasional fasting, you can follow your straight and narrow path to heaven. Have confidence in My help and your faith will set you free of the bondage of sin."*

Saturday, May 1, 1999:

At St. Michael's Church, Roscommon, Michigan, after Communion, I could see Jesus suffering on the cross with His crown of thorns. There were snakes crawling all over Him trying to hide Him on the cross. Jesus said: *"My people, I love you so much that I died for the forgiveness of your sins. You have been redeemed by My suffering on the cross. You cannot have My Easter Resurrection unless you remember the price I paid for you on the cross.*

So display My Crucifix with the Corpus in your churches and in your homes, so you will never forget how much I love you. The snakes all over Me represent how Satan and the demons want you to forget My Crucifixion and they want you to remove My Crucifixes out of sight. I have given you an example in My earthly suffering that you too will have to endure the trials of life. You will experience love and joy, but you will witness hatred and sorrow as well. Think of your life as picking up your own cross and carrying it to Calvary. Once you have suffered your Good Friday for My Name's sake, you will be raised up in your resurrection one day as well. I have promised to bring you to Heaven, if you are faithful in following My Will. I created every soul to be with Me in Heaven, so you can share in My love. It is your free will choice to love Me in return. I reach out to forgive every soul of their sins, so come and share in My eternal love in Heaven."

Sunday, May 2, 1999:

At St. Michael's Church, Roscommon, Michigan, after Communion, I could see a bare cross and then I could see the roof of a Church from the inside. Jesus said: *"My people, this cross is bare because it awaits each of you to pick it up and carry it through life. You have walked with Me through the Gospels on My way to Calvary. Now, I am walking with you on your road to Heaven. Never fear the trials of life, because I am at your side waiting for you to call on My help. I have asked you to take My yoke upon your shoulders, for My burden is light. For those that follow My Will, you will be blessed in many beautiful ways of the Spirit. As My apostles were strengthened by the Holy Spirit, you too are enabled through your Confirmation in the Spirit as well. I showed you in the vision of the roof of this church, because I am depending on My faithful to build up My Church with many conversions. It is not enough to be thankful for your gift of faith, but you must share My Gospel message with those around you. Every time you reach out in love to share My Word, the Holy Spirit will give you what to proclaim. Rejoice in My love and the fellowship of your faith with your friends and relatives. You will one day see the beauty of sharing in the communion of saints that all of My faithful can look forward to share with Me in*

Heaven. You may struggle for a short time on earth, but My faithful will then enjoy the infinite love and peace I will wrap around you in Heaven."

Monday, May 3, 1999:

At St. Mary's Queen of Creation, New Baltimore, Michigan, after Communion, I could see a flower open up and there was a large city with lights at night. This scene pulled out further to see the shape of the United States. Jesus said: *"My people of America, your cities are in the darkness of your sins. As you read in the Scriptures of the evils of the people of Noah's day and that of Sodom and Gomorrah, do not think you are any better. A time is coming when I will rain down My wrath of judgment on your land. You continue to commit sins of abortion and the sins of the flesh. You have lost your knowledge of sinful behavior, because you see things through the eyes of the world instead of the eyes of faith. Many of you do not think of yourself as sinners in need of repentance. For those who are not following My Will, they will see My swift justice as the comet will consume them. As you saw Me cleanse the earth of all evil by water and fire in the past, you will see the earth purified once again. Prepare your souls in Confession of your sins so you will be like the wise virgins ready to receive Me. The foolish virgins are the unfaithful who will be barred from My banquet, as they will wail and gnash their teeth in the eternal darkness of Hell."*

Later, at Adoration, I could see a Host in a monstrance and a dove representing the Holy Spirit flew out of the Host. Jesus said: *"My people, the Holy Spirit is present wherever you witness My Real Presence. As you recognize Me in the breaking of the bread, your brokenness is strengthened by the grace of My sacrament. You are weak in your sins because of Adam's sin. Your brokenness comes from your weakened state from the effects of original sin. I came to die for your sins and give you My Body and Blood to heal your brokenness. Come and follow Me in My plan for your life and you will be made complete. I take your broken heart of sin and mend it in Confession, so your soul can be radiant again. By a faithful love of Me and following My Will, I will raise up your soul after death in a glorified body which will be devoid of your weaknesses. You will then experience the perfection that Adam enjoyed before he fell in sin. Once all the effects of sin are removed, you will be in full joy of seeing Me in Heaven with infinite love and a peace beyond your dreams."*

Tuesday, May 4, 1999:

After Communion, I could see a pew with a pair of glasses sitting on it. Jesus said: *"My people, many of you are spiritually blinded by the cares and pleasures of the world. Just as you require glasses at times to see things more clearly, you also need the eyes of faith to see spiritually as well. Look beyond the earthly desires of the body and seek first those things that will benefit your soul most. The world is passing away, but your soul lives on forever. When you study My Scriptures and follow My Will, you will understand how to save your soul. By loving Me and your neighbor, you will have the foundation of how to live and please Me. Do not let your own pride and agenda cloud your path to Heaven, but shine My light of grace on your path to see Me clearly. When you view life with love, you are able to reach out and share your time and your goods with others. When you view life selfishly, you will do things only for yourself and you will not see to help others. That is why your perspective of life is so important. Pray, My children, for discernment so you can understand how to focus on My ways through the glasses of faith."*

Later, at Adoration, I could see a woman teacher pointing a metal detector at those entering the school. Jesus said: *"My people, you have reached a new level of terrorism when you have to be concerned about your children carrying weapons. How many lives are going to be lost in your schools until your society wakes up to what your children are being exposed to? The violence on TV and in your movies has been a plague beyond pornography. Your computer age has given too much information to those who want to destroy and kill. You have become a violent people with homicides at a high level and many abortions every day. Wars are ongoing in many countries at any one time. Is it any wonder that such a violent culture will breed children killing each other? Turn off your televisions and boycott your violent movies and you will take away the money from those perpetrating violence. Stop your*

*wars and killing babies and you will take the blood money away
from the arms makers and the doctors. You need to pray much to
protect your families from being infected with your anger driven
death culture. If you could instill a proper moral character in
your children by going to church and having a daily prayer life,
you would be on your way to a more peaceful society. You have to
start with love and let love permeate everything you do in order to
eradicate the hate in many souls. Call on Me to help spread love
throughout your world and you could have a lasting peace."*

Wednesday, May 5, 1999:

After Communion, I could see someone kneeling in a pew.
Jesus said: *"My people, I give you a quotation from Phillipians
2:9-10. 'Therefore God also has exalted Him and has bestowed
upon Him the name that is above every name, so that at the name
of Jesus every knee should bend of those in Heaven, on earth,
and under the earth.' This is the reverence I seek from you at the
sound of My Name. I ask you also to kneel before My Real Presence at the Consecration of the Mass. When you pass by My Eucharist in the Tabernacle, I ask you to genuflect in giving Me
praise and adoration. I am with you at all times and I am Lord
over the universe. I have given you free will to love and adore
Me. You have a choice to give Me reverence or not, but if you love
Me, you would honor My request. As you prepare to come to
Heaven, you could honor Me as the angels do by kneeling in
prayer and adoration. When you are in Heaven, your praise of
Me will never cease. So even while you are on earth, you can
imitate the angels. When you kneel to Me in homage, I will bless
you for your faithfulness."*

Later, at Adoration, I could see a monstrance in the dark with a
light on the background. Jesus said: *"My people, you have focused
on your worldly things while I am not even thought about. You
have put Me out of sight at church and out of your minds as well.
Your extended affluence has lulled you to sleep so much that you
do not even recognize how evil you have become. You have all the
material things that you need, such that you forget who gave you
all of your blessings to begin with. Many of you are lukewarm or
not even attending church. Wake up and see that your morals*

have fallen apart and you are headed to ruin by your own hands. Now is the acceptable time to reform your lives and your society. Your weather chastisements and your wars are only interrupting your comforts and pleasures. You do not see these things as a result of your sins. A time is coming quickly when you will be tested by the evil of the coming tribulation. Those, who do not seek My help, will be lost. So prepare now with repentance and daily prayer so you will be able to withstand the onslaught of the Antichrist and the demons. With My help and that of your guardian angel, your soul will be saved."

Thursday, May 6, 1999:

After Communion, I could see a huge wall of water cascading over some skyscrapers in a coastal city. Jesus said: *"My people, a day is coming when My justice will be carried out on your world for their non-compromising sins. My comet of chastisement will be My triumph over evil that no one will be able to defy. This event will end your tribulation and will be the means by which I will cleanse the earth again of all evil spirits and evil people. I will protect My faithful through all of this disaster. The unfaithful will suffer dearly as they will all be cast into Hell. All of the warning messages, I have given you, are in preparation for My glorious coming. You must repent now of your sins before My hand falls against the evil of the earth. A time of tribulation will come about, but My power will quickly vanquish Satan and his demons. The evil of your world has gone beyond the point of no return as in the time of Noah. Prepare your spiritual lives and be ready to receive Me as I will come in triumph."*

Later, at the prayer group, I could see a crucifix taken down and laying on the ground. Jesus said: *"My people, many of My Crucifixes have been taken down or have never even been put up in your churches or homes. I have stressed to You before about the importance of My Crucifix being displayed. you have in that moment on the cross the ultimate expression of Divine love for man. This is your sign of redemption. It is also a sign of suffering that all Christians should be willing to endure for My Name's sake. I have shown you My love. Can you give Me your love in return?"*

I could see some roses before a smiling mother. Jesus said: *"My people, you are honoring your mothers this week for all they do for the family. The mother is the heart and focal point of your families. Pray for them and thank them that you were not aborted. Other mothers, who aborted their children, will never see them again in this life. Pray also to your heavenly mother Mary for all of her intentions in this month of May that honors her."*

I could see some beautiful foods and desserts. Jesus said: *"My people, you have been fortunate in America to have all the food you need. Many have even grown overweight because of your excesses and poor diets. Think of those who do not even have enough to eat and go starving every night. Have pity on those in need of food and help them with your time and your money. At your judgment feeding the hungry will be one of your tests. If you feed the poor, you are feeding Me in them."*

I could see some people fighting in the desert. Jesus said: *"My people, why do you persist in your incessant wars? Destruction is the only result from war. Killing and bombing makes no sense in a Christian life. Peace comes from compromising peacemakers and prayer. Gaining your own selfish objectives should not be reason for your wars. You should struggle to live peaceably with your neighbor, instead of forcing him to live by your ideas. You keep repeating history in your wars of futility. Learn to love your neighbor and war will not be an option."*

I could see some friends visiting each other with a light coming from the door. Jesus said: *"My people, reach out in friendship to your neighbors by sharing what you have with others. Be willing to open your home to someone in need. In other words help your neighbor as you would expect them to help you. Reach out to your friends in sharing your spiritual bounty as well. Encourage your friends to see My love and welcome them into the faith. You will be judged also on how you reached out to save souls."*

I could see some new homes and then the devastation of your tornadoes. Jesus said: *"My people, you have seen much loss of life and homes destroyed in your latest weather testing. Even some are starting to question if God is causing these storms as a chastisement. The deeper connection between your sins and these storms would be closer to the truth, but many people do not want to believe they are sinners. Instead, you rationalize your sins as some other cause than yourselves. Wake up to the truth of your actions and seek to repent of your sins. You have a lifetime to perfect your spiritual lives. Use your time wisely for your soul's benefit, because your time is running out."*

I could see the inside of a house that was simply furnished. Jesus said: *"My people, you need to live simpler lives without all of your rich furnishings. You can lead simple lives if you choose. Instead of buying only the best and keeping up with your neighbor, you should be working on gaining heavenly riches. You can do this with acts of charity and corporal works of mercy without being asked. Live to please Me in following My Will and you will have more than enough to do. Be grateful for what little you have instead of seeking to pile up elusive wealth."*

Friday, May 7, 1999:

After Communion, I could look down on an open can for food that was empty. Jesus said: *"My people, you will be happy to have any canned food available when your famine and computer problems begin. You are comfortable now and many are unaware how quickly things are going to change. You cannot imagine how chaotic people will get when their food supplies are threatened. That is why I have been encouraging you to make an attempt to store one year's supply of food and water. I will multiply food for My faithful, so do not worry about sharing with others. The more people prepare now, the easier your transition will be to your lack of power and transportation. Many have their heads buried in the sand of only today's worries. Heed My warnings, for if you doubt them, you will be in deep need. Think of the starving refugees and how you would have to deal with no more food at the stores. I am giving you the grace to be forewarned about these events. Pray for discernment in what you should do."*

Later, at Adoration, I could see a maroon velvet chair of power that was empty. Jesus said: *"My people, your leaders are proud and enjoying the power they command. They all are joined in trying to control the world by their commands. They will be double crossed by the Antichrist who will subtly usurp their power and dispose of them in his lies. That is why these seats of power will be empty, as the Antichrist will appoint his own heads of state. Even as the Antichrist comes to full power over the earth, his reign will be brief also. My triumph will come quickly to cast all of the evil spirits and evil people into Hell. Those, that think they will have it easy by taking the Mark of the Beast, will suffer the most on earth and in Hell. You will then see even the throne of the Antichrist empty as he will have to give in to My power. I am allowing this tribulation as a test of your faith. Those, who seek My help and believe in My Name, will see My glory in Heaven and on earth. Do not seek fame and power in this world since it lasts but a moment in time. Seek heavenly things which are everlasting."*

Saturday, May 8, 1999:

After Communion, I could see a large arch of stone with water running underneath it. Jesus said: *"My son, you have been reading in the Scriptures of St. Paul's many travels in his missionary work. He was limited in some of his preaching by persecutions in many places that did not want to hear My Name. You, yourself, will gradually be limited in your travels by increasing persecution as well. The more you proclaim My Word and save souls in My name, the more they will persecute you. All of your suffering of criticism will be the price of the souls saved. You have realized this price of souls in many of your trials. I am warning you now that this persecution will increase until it will be difficult to travel anywhere. As your world grows more evil in its ways, the people's hearts will become so hardened that they will refuse to listen to My Word or anyone proclaiming My Word. As you approach the end of this year, travel itself will become more difficult both in the air and on the ground. Your world will be visited by a disaster in your computer problems. This will be the fulfillment of how your technology will bring about your own destruction. It is appropriate that man's pride will be humbled by his own imperfections. Your way of life will change dramatically and it will open you to the opportunity of the Antichrist's takeover."*

Later, I could see a baptismal font with a spotlight shining on it giving long shadows. Jesus said: *"My people, many of you were Baptized as infants when you were brought into My Church. It was your parents and godparents who spoke up for you in making your vows to be faithful in obeying My Commandments and renouncing Satan. It is up to you parents to see to the religious education of each child by bringing each child to Sunday Mass*

and teaching them the truths of the faith. Your responsibility does not end after their school years. You should encourage your children to follow their faith even during their adult years by your example and gentle advice. The children are responsible for their souls as they come of age, but they still may wander away without any guidance. There are many worldly distractions, but each soul will still have to answer for their life's actions at the judgment. You mothers are being honored this week for bringing your children into the world. See that you do everything in your power to save your children's souls before they leave this world."

Sunday, May 9, 1999: (Mother's Day)

After Communion, I could see the Blessed Virgin Mary come with her blue mantle stretched out. Mary said: *"My dear children, today is a fitting day for mothers to love their children, and for the children to thank their mothers for the gift of life. I come today as well to pour out my love on all of my children. I bring you my mantle of protection as my Son and I will not leave you orphans. Many times my Son told you to have no fear as He greeted His apostles with: 'Peace be with you.' Call on my intercession and my Son's graces will see you through your everyday trials. Be joyful that you have such heavenly guardians as Jesus and myself. When you pray my Rosary, think of all the people of the world that I desire to watch over. I love you, my children, and I want you to love each other."*

Monday, May 10, 1999:

After Communion, I could see some modern stores and buildings inside. Jesus said: *"My people, no matter how confident you become in your modern technology, your knowledge will never come close to complete. Your computers will take you only so far, but these are still only worldly distractions from your real purpose on earth. There has been no change over history in the real confrontation of concern over saving your soul. The battle of good and evil has gone on for years and still you are dealing with the same adversary in Satan. I have been here to save you and help you, if you would only listen to My ways instead of your own. If you do not follow My Will, you will continue to repeat the history of your mistakes. My place is in everyone of your lives. It is up to you to recognize what happens when you take Me out of your sight. When you let Me run your lives, everything else will fall into place. Seek My love and the forgiveness of your sins and you will save your soul. Your eternal salvation is the only thing of importance here."*

Later, at Adoration, I could see many spotlights falling on the darkness of the earth. Jesus said: *"My people, as you live and breathe each day, all Heaven is watching your every move. Every soul is in the spotlight of life. You are scrutinized by Me, the angels and the saints. That is why it is so important for each of you to live your faith and give good example to all of those around you. In addition to heaven watching you, all of humanity is watching your every move and listening to your every word. You can be a good example or a bad example by your actions. So be a positive influence on others and seek to follow My Commandments, if you are to be saved. Make My laws and My life's example a part of your life by taking them to heart. You will have failures because of your sinful nature. But seek My forgiveness of your sins in Confession so you can refocus your path to Heaven. I love all of you so much and I want you to live in My Divine Will. Pray and struggle to give witness to Me in all that you do on earth. Other souls will recognize your love for Me and they will want to share in your fervor of faith. Be leaders in following Me and by your good example you will lead souls to Me. You are in a great harvest of souls in an evil age. Do not give in to the comforts of the world, but walk proud in your faith giving constant witness to My love before all those on earth and in Heaven."*

Tuesday, May 11, 1999:

After Communion, I could see a large metallic nosecone housing nuclear bombs. Jesus said: *"My people, with all of your recent violence using handguns, you are seeking to restrict them. Most uses of your handguns are for killing people. The same can be said for making nuclear bombs, only they are meant to kill millions of people. As you discuss the divulging of this secret information on making warheads, consider more the spread of these devices around the world. You are in armed camps with a poten-*

tial war possible that could destroy all of mankind from the fall-out of many bombs. With more countries possessing such weapons, why do you not take this threat more seriously? Many times prayers for peace have been requested, especially to stop the use of such mass destruction weapons. You have lived in the shadow of an atomic war for years, but you have become apathetic to such a possibility since it has not happened. Remember that as Satan's time is running out, he will try to inspire the most killing of man that he can. So pray much to stop the use of these atomic weapons which threaten your survival more than ever. Understand the real threat of evil people holding their fingers on this nuclear trigger. Literally your lives depend on how much prayer that you can storm Heaven for peace in your world. Do not forget to pray for this intention every day."

Later, at Adoration, I could see a large room with velvet sofas, but each end had narrow doors. Jesus said: *"My people, many of you are comfortable in your homes and are not concerned over possible shortages or the coming tribulation. Just as people are comfortable in this room, when the alarms sound, it will be difficult to exit this room in a time of trouble. You will see a coming time of trials as early as the end of this year. While some are preparing for power outages, others are not heeding any of the warnings of this time. You will need spiritual preparation for the coming trials, because basic instincts may drive people to irrational behavior. You need to be loving and not selfish even in a time of need. Your preparations of prayer and material things will even help your desperate neighbors. The most important of all of your preparations is to keep your trust in Me, no matter what you will be faced with. Do not rely on weapons, because those who use them, will die by them. When you pour out love on someone in need, they will be more at ease and not in a panic. Encourage My children in their yearly preparations so they will not be found wanting. You have been given ample time to prepare for this coming trial, so move forward in your preparations."*

Wednesday, May 12, 1999:

After Communion, I could look down on a train traveling forward on its tracks. Jesus said: *"My people, when you look on your spiritual path to Heaven, you should think of it as this train moving forward. Your spiritual life cannot be stagnant in one spot. It must be vibrant and improving every day. Check your progress each day to see if you are gaining or losing. Build on your previous failures by correcting them and strive to keep from falling back into your old habits of the flesh. The more you work on improving your spiritual life, the closer you will come to Me in love. Look to My life for a goal to imitate. Seek to gain in heavenly riches by your kind deeds and gifts to your neighbor. Do not be selfish, but share what you have with others. In all that you do, let yourself be led by love of God and love of neighbor."*

Later, at Adoration, I could see an old windmill used to pump water up out of the ground. Jesus said: *"My people, many of your old devices may be more useful to you when you will be concerned about power outages. People in days gone by had many ways to get by without all of your modern day reliance on electricity. You may be forced to use your old devices for heat and light. I have warned you before in messages how your standard of living would be reduced to a more primitive way of life, because of the failure of your technology. You will be humbled by your computer problems and your creature comforts will be stripped from you. Prepare now to do with less and build up your spiritual stamina for when you will be tested by Satan and his demons. Call on My help to get you through these earthly trials so you can enjoy the heavenly peace of My Era of Peace."*

Thursday, May 13, 1999: (Ascension Thursday)

After Communion, I could see Jesus ascending into heaven in bright white robes. Jesus said: *"My people, as I left My disciples, I encouraged them to wait until they received power from the Holy Spirit. They were saddened that I was leaving, but they could not be empowered by the Holy Spirit until I left. As I taught My disciples to go out and preach My Gospel to all of the nations, I give that same command to all of My faithful. You also, have been empowered by the Holy Spirit through your Baptism and Confirmation. To do My work of evangelization, you must constantly protect your prayer life with prayer and fasting. It is from My strength and that of the Holy Spirit that We may speak through you and give you what to say. All the blessings and graces that go out to convert souls come through you, My instruments. It is proper to give thanks and praise to God for even one person who converts their life to following Me. I have told you many times how Heaven rejoices over the saving of even one soul. Rejoice in the gift of faith that each of you have received and continue to nurture and sustain your love for Me."*

Later, at the prayer group, I could see a brief red image of Satan attacking the earth. Jesus said: *"My people, you should be aware of Satan's attacks on My churches, your families and your leaders. First of all, Satan is a real fallen angel and he is encouraging sin in the world. This is an evil age and it very well fits the description of Noah's day in the end times. People have lost their sense of sin and there is not enough love in your world both for Me and your neighbor. Because of this evil world, you need My help more than ever. Come to Me in prayer and Confession and I will direct you on your way to Heaven."*

I could see a child in a kitchen and he held an empty food can. Jesus said: *"My children, I have given you many messages concerning the storage of one year's supply of food and water. Many have criticized this message, but these people do not understand that this warning is to allow you time to prepare. When the famine and the control of your food limits your access to food, how are you going to answer your starving children? I have not given this message to be popular or to ease those seeking to be politically appeasing to the people. This is a difficult message, but one you need to be forewarned so you can help your relatives and your neighbors."*

I could see some cartoons displaying violent killings. Jesus said: *"My people, you are naively discussing the causes of your recent school killings. You claim there should be a free right of speech to have pornography in public, but you are aghast at your many raped women. Your violent movies and computer games will continue to be sold by those making money with no concern for the effects on the children's minds. You have many causes of this violence in children, but it starts with the lack of love and poor example from the parents. If you spent time showing concern for your children and taught them how to pray in the family, your violent children would be very few."*

I could see a child's face and a time line of their growing up. Jesus said: *"My people, you parents have the most influence in how your children are raised. Lead them to Me through love. If your children only see you in angry reprimands, they will not know your love. Hold them and show them that you care about their lives. I have given you examples in the lives of the Holy Family. Imitate Us in your families and you will have a peace that other families do not have when I am not present."*

I could see a family in recreation together. Jesus said: *"My people, in order to have more harmony and love in your families, you need to involve every member in your activities. When you pray together and play together, you are giving good example for how your children will bring up their own families. If you have division when each does their own activity, how can you have unity and avoid divorce? Work together as a team with a proper balance of love of Me and each other and you will have a lasting family life."*

I could see a small town street with shops and homes. Jesus said: *"My people, if you are looking for cities and towns without killings and drugs, you need to examine the health of your families. You have many broken homes with divorce, many couples living together and some homosexual marriages. Is there any wonder why your society is in the shape it is? Live according to My Commandments and not in adultery, fornication, or homosexual sins. Then your cities will cleanse themselves of the evil influence of your sins and you will have examples for your children to follow."*

I could see some gun turrets of soldiers at war. Jesus said: *"My people, when you replace love in your families with hate and extend this to your ethnic groups and nations, wars will result. Wars are the symptoms of the hate and sins in your world. You need to spread My message of love in the Gospel to all the nations if you expect to have peace in your world. You are in the midst of a battle of good and evil. Do everything in your power through prayer to bring love of God and neighbor to those around you. If each family contributed their love to the world, you would not have these wars."*

Friday, May 14, 1999:

After Communion, I could see some modern lights turned off. Jesus said: *"My people, I have asked you to prepare both physically and spiritually for the coming tribulation. While you have been getting your mind around these coming events, the Antichrist and his agents have been making their own preparations as well. This light is to indicate how soon he is ready to assume power and how he will use all of your technology for his advantage. You will see a man of lies and charisma try to win over people to his thinking as a man of peace. He will have demonic powers in using miracles and illusions to persuade people that he is the Christ and even greater. Do not believe in anyone claiming to be Me, for I will come in glory on the clouds and no one will be able to deny My day of triumph. Call on Me in prayer and fasting, for you will need My help and that of your guardian angel. Do not be fearful of what is to come, but have faith that My power is greater than the Antichrist. I am permitting this test of your faith, but you will not be tested beyond your endurance. I am speaking of this trial so you will know of its coming, but be assured of My miraculous intervention. I will provide My faithful with all that you will need. I will even shorten the time of your trial for the sake of My elect. Stay close to Me in prayer and keep your hearts united with My love. In all that you will face, continue to trust in My Name, even if it may require your life in martyrdom."*

Later, at St. John Neuman Adoration, Houston, Texas, I could see an altar with a shield representing a goddess of fertility. Jesus said: *"My people, in your modern days you still have some that are giving homage to pagan gods. This goddess to fertility refers both to crops and having children. Even though some believe in a higher force, they still do not want to believe in the one true God. Those of the New Age movement believe in the gods of nature of the earth. This same group is promoting a One World religion that will be supported by the United Nations and soon by the Antichrist. I have come in person to reveal to you what the Father has given Me. I am true love and it is by My authority that all creation obeys Me, even as I calmed the storm. It is the Creator that you should worship and not the attributes of creation. I* am your God and believe in Me only. Do not follow anyone who claims to be Me or a ruler of this world. The Antichrist and Satan are conspiring to mislead you with their lies and miracles. Follow only Me and you will be saved through My power. When they come to force their Mark of the Beast on you, refuse any of their goods and jobs and refuse to worship the Beast or take his Mark. Love Me only and I will provide for your needs. Be forewarned of this evil tribulation that will test your faith. With Me at your side, you will have nothing to fear."

Saturday, May 15, 1999:

At St. Helen's, Pearland, Texas, I could see a New Age building with many strange shapes. Jesus said: *"My people, beware of the false christs and those worshiping alien gods in these end days. Some will even come in My Name and try to have you worship them or gods of the earth. No matter how attractive their words are or how many miracles they will perform, believe in Me only. There will be many promoting a One World religion that will be worshiping the gods of the earth. You have Me as the Creator and I alone should you worship. Stay faithful to following My Commandments and follow My pope son, John Paul II. I love you very much and I do not want to see any of My faithful misled by these false teachers. Follow your prayer life and the sacraments for as long as you have faithful priests. There will come a time when you will no longer have Mass available. Then you will rely on your prayer groups and spiritual communion. Keep close to Me at all times and you will be protected."*

Sunday, May 16, 1999:

At Queen of Peace, Houston, Texas, after Communion, I could see all races and nationalities lined up to receive Holy Communion at a Mass. Jesus said: *"My people, I welcome everyone from all walks of life to come forward in faith to be a part of My Mystical Body. When you all receive Me in Holy Communion, you are joined as one in My Body and Blood. Give Me thanks and praise for all that I have done for each of you. I have given you a gift of life, a gift of faith, and a sharing in My death and Resurrection. As you look on the cross where I died, this is the most precious* gift of My life that I have given up for you and your sins. All that you are and all that you have are gifts to you for your faithfulness. Do not be prideful in your own deeds and accomplishments, for I have given you the abilities and the resources for what you have done. Giving Me thanks in Holy Communion is an acknowledgment of My graces and an understanding of your place in creation. You have free will and it is your choice to love Me and follow My Will. Those, who follow My path to Heaven, rejoice to be a part of My Mystical Body and do everything to show their love for Me. I bless all of you for listening to My Word and carrying out My plan for your life."*

Monday, May 17, 1999: (Funeral Mass for Pat Flood, my uncle)

After Communion, I could see Pat and Adelaide with a unity candle. Jesus said: *"My dear friends, in this vision I am showing you how Patrick was greeted by his wife, who has been waiting for him. He has had a full and blessed life for the joy and love that he has brought to all those whom he knew. Take a moment to dwell on how he has touched each of your lives. Now the two of them are joined once again as indicated in the unity candle in the vision. They will be praying for all of their family members as you remember each of them this day. They are beautiful examples in life for you to follow. Continue to walk on your own road to Calvary with your heads lifted high in love and not in sorrow."*

Later, at Adoration, I could see a small roadside shrine with a candle burning. Then I saw some other shrines on the road and some tornadoes. Jesus said: *"My people, I have shown you how quickly your life can be taken by a sudden car accident or a violent weather storm. It is possible some souls could be lost to the evil one if they were caught unaware of their immediate death. That is why it is so important to always have your souls in the state of sanctifying grace. If you should fall into serious sin, waste no time in getting to Confession. Be in constant preparation to receive Me, because you know not the hour I will call you home. You could die before these final events of the tribulation. When you are in constant prayer adoring Me and giving Me thanks, you will be preparing yourself for Heaven. The angels sing their endless praise and thanksgiving to My glory. By being ready to receive Me at any time, you would be ready to die even if you should die suddenly."*

Tuesday, May 18, 1999:

After Communion, I could see many precious gems in a glass case. Jesus said: *"My people, your souls are like priceless gems beyond any earthly value. You cannot be replaced for any amount of money. That is why each soul is so precious to Me and should be precious to you. Life is a gift that you have only one opportunity to accept. It does not matter whether you are a king or the lowliest servant, you are equally important in My eyes. Because your life is irreplaceable, that is why any taking of life is the worst sin you could commit against My Commandments. Why has your society put a cheap price on life? If an infant is inconvenient to you, your laws allow you to abort a pregnancy in killing your baby. You are even trying to kill anyone in pain through euthanasia. When life is so cheapened, even killing in war is made accidental. If you thought life is as precious as I do, you would do everything possible to preserve life in all of its stages. If you all loved one another as you should, you would not even contemplate wars for things or control. Share this love I have with all people so they may come to know the true value and preciousness of each life. Pray to stop your killing in abortions, wars, or murders. If you do not change your ways, you may threaten man's very survival."*

Later, at Adoration, I could see a ship with red, blue and white colors out on the ocean and there were some large clouds coming over the ship. Jesus said: *"My people of America, you will continue to see violent storms and disasters all over your land. You are not heeding My warnings to repent of your sins and change your ways. Because you are not listening to My pleas, you will continue to be stripped of your possessions. You work many hours to try and gain the pleasures of life, but your desires are being frustrated by the destruction before you. Because both parents are working, your children are not getting enough of your attention. It is important for mothers to take care of their preschoolers at home. The few extra things you work for are not worth the love you can give your children by your presence. It is because your children do not see you, that they look for attention in other ways. That is why many parents do not know what their children are doing. The wayward children of your evil age are being too influenced by Satan's working on their minds through TV and other violent distractions. Be involved with your children's spiritual and secular training or your children will grow up as strangers in your midst. Pray for the children and the parents so your families will be united with My love. Without Me in your lives, many families will become divided."*

Wednesday, May 19, 1999:

After Communion, I could see an earthly king and his court. Jesus said: *"My people, do not aspire to fame and fortune in this life. It is only by pride and greed for wealth that many seek positions of authority and the possession of earthly things. Instead of the low road of earthly desires, seek the high road of heavenly treasures. When you share your time and wealth with others, you are giving back your due in thanksgiving for My many blessings upon you. Keep your gaze fixed on following My example, and you will be following My Will. Those, who follow their own agenda and satisfy their earthly pleasures, will get caught up in the snares of the evil one. By following My Commandments and restraining your desires through self control, you will be on the right road to following My plan for your life. When you give in to following My Will, you will see love leading you to helping others and less concern for any of your selfish desires."*

Later, at Adoration, I could see an upside down picture of people in a park. Jesus said: *"My people, when I came upon the earth, I turned the thinking at that time upside down. Some were forcing others to obey the letter of the law, while I was encouraging My faithful to follow the spirit of the law. I came to fulfill all of the Scriptures that spoke of a Redeemer and a Messiah. I spoke of a New Commandment of love, yet it was the same love that inspired Moses and My disciples. I spoke of forgiving your neighbor seventy times seven times. I spoke of loving your enemies and turning your cheek again after being struck. I spoke of the beatitudes in how to live your life of prayer. These were difficult messages in My day, but no more difficult than in your own day. Your world is in an evil age and preaching repentance of your sins is still falling on deaf ears. Reach out as I did in My day to save as many souls as you can. Many converted on hearing My words. So I am asking your prayers through the Holy Spirit to touch those hearts willing to listen to My Words. My call of love goes out to all the nations to stop their evil ways and follow My path to Heaven."*

Thursday, May 20, 1999:
After Communion, I could see someone in a yellow life raft. Jesus said: *"My people, you are seeing in this life raft how important this could be to save yourself from a sinking ship. In the physical world you understand the threat to your life from drowning in the ocean. In your spiritual life you should be more aware of how dangerous it is to be drowning in your sins. Sin can be a gradual thing that you do not even recognize when your spiritual life is endangered. If you take time each night to evaluate your day's actions, you can see for yourself if you are falling into deeper sins. When you are overwhelmed by temptations and your sinful habits, reach out for My help in prayer and confess your sins to the priest. Think of My graces and blessings as a spiritual life raft to keep you from drowning in your sins. Your spiritual life is much more important than your physical life. You should be paying attention to sins that threaten your spiritual life so you can avoid them and save your soul. Reach out to your neighbors as well to help them with My spiritual rafts of protection. Let Me rescue you in your need and I will guide you on your voyage to heaven."*

Later, at the prayer group, I could see a school setting with a gunsight focused on the school. Jesus said: *"My people, how quickly have you revisited more violence in your schools. The blessing of this latest event was that no one was killed. This is another sign that your children's emotions have resorted to violence. Satan is influencing many of your young people through the adult examples that they imitate. The violence on your news reporting of wars all over the world has shown up your society's double standard. On one hand you tell your children not to shoot someone, yet they see the hypocrisy in your abortions and killing in war. When your children see a peaceful world, then they will not have evil examples to follow.”*

I could see a yellow light in the sky and God the Father said: *“I AM shares with you in your preparations for your conference in My honor. I will usher in many blessings on those who attend. In every way possible share with each other how My graces have affected your lives. The faithful remnant will have to carry My Church through the coming tribulation. So build on these three years of Pope John Paul II’s plan for your jubilee celebration. Call on My help as your tribulation draws near.”*

I could see the wings on an angel and I asked Jesus for per-

mission for my angel, Mark, to speak. Mark said: *"My dear child, the angels of Heaven and your guardian angels are preparing for the coming last battle between good and evil. The days of your tribulation are not far off. You should be preparing your soul spiritually in prayer for your coming fight with the demons. You will see Jesus' heavenly triumph come as He defeats Satan and the Antichrist at the Battle of Armageddon. Have no fear, but rejoice that His victory will be complete as the evil ones are cast into Hell."*

I could see many heads bowed as the Holy Spirit came in flames of fire to inspire those faithful to Jesus' Word. Jesus said: *"My people, you are about to celebrate Pentecost on Sunday. See that all of you have been given the gifts of the Holy Spirit in Baptism and Confirmation. His power is the wind that passes through your soul. With His help all of My faithful will have the strength to step out in faith to witness to Me, even when they persecute you for believing in My Name."*

I could see a man with a small light searching to investigate those stealing your nuclear secrets. I then saw a picture of the four horsemen of the Apocalypse. Jesus said: *"My people, as more of your nuclear secrets are seen in a new light of investigation, you will wonder why your government has not punished these spies. Your government leaders have sold out your people and they are afraid to admit their treason. That is why many are trying to cover up these thefts with politics. In essence your leaders have unleashed atomic weapons information to all countries who desire to have these weapons. Pray every day that these weapons never get used."*

I could see a large hill of mud moving forward to engulf some villages. Jesus said: *"My people, you have seen many disasters in your weather events this year. I am showing you one more destruction by mud and floods that will test your people. You have failed to repent of your sins. So you will continue to see these weather chastisements strip your possessions."*

I could see someone drawing a game on a window. Jesus said: *"My people, as you look at the seats of power in all of your nations, there is very little change in the control of these countries. You are faced with no alternatives in your leaders because they are all under the control of the One World bankers. It is your debts and central banks that really dictate your future behind the scenes. These are a part of the control of your world that will be handed over to the Antichrist when he assumes power. These evil ones have been preparing for this world takeover for many years. Just as they think they have won, I will smite them with My victory. You will not see true justice until I come again."*

Friday, May 21, 1999:

After Communion, I could see an empty chair and sense a time of persecution. Jesus said: *"My people, in the readings you have seen how St. Peter and St. Paul were imprisoned and persecuted for speaking out in My Name.... A religious persecution is coming for all of My faithful. You may be called on to witness to Me even when your life may be endangered for doing so. Call on My help and that of the Holy Spirit for what to do and say during this trial. You all will be tested in your belief in Me. No one will be spared this persecution. You all will have to struggle and suffer for My Name's sake. Rest assured that My angels will assist you and have no fear, since My victory will come soon. Bear with your persecution for a while and you soon will be rewarded for your faithfulness. Those, who refuse to follow Me, will suffer much more than My faithful. Those, seeking to avoid being persecuted by taking the Mark of the Beast, will suffer a hell on earth and an eternal hellfire as well. This time will test your faith so much, that without My help you will lose your soul. The lukewarm and those, who cannot make a decision, will be swept away by Satan, if they do not convert their lives. Prepare your prayer lives so you will be able to withstand this coming persecution."*

Saturday, May 22, 1999:

At St. John's Church, Westminister, Maryland, after Communion, I could see an oval shaped window in a Church with a bright morning sunlight shining through the window. Jesus said: *"My people, I am an all loving God and I shine My love and graces on you every day. All I ask is that you open your heart so I can shine My light of love on you. When you share with Me in prayer and in Holy Communion, I swell up the tears of joy in your heart. My surge of love is overwhelming because I love you so much. You can show your love for Me in everything you do each day by consecrating them up to Me as a prayer. Then all that you do that day I will receive from you and I will store it in your heavenly treasury. I am the light of the world and I seek to be a part of everyone's life. I am love personified and I am full truth knowing everything. I invite all of you to be a part of My Mystical Body. Windows can be opened to the light or you can draw the shades to stop the light. Do not be selfish with your love and keep it from Me, but keep your hearts open as this window, so My love can constantly burn in your hearts. When all of you are focused on My light, reach out to share the joy of My love with your neighbors so they can open their hearts to Me also. Your life is too short to live it in sorrow. Be joyful because My love permeates through all of My creation. Lift up your hearts and share every day in the joy of My love. Those, who put love in all they do, will one day enjoy their eternal love with Me in Heaven."*

Sunday, May 23, 1999: (Pentecost Sunday)

At St. Joseph's Church, in Taneytown, Maryland, after Communion, I could see Jesus on the cross and then a dove with its wings open above the cross. I then saw a hearth of fire emanating from the heart of Jesus and Mary. The Holy Spirit said: *"I am the Spirit of Love and I come in your hearts today on My feast day of Pentecost. As Jesus breathed My Presence upon His disciples, I came in a great wind to the apostles in the upper room. It was then that My tongues of fire came over them and enabled them to speak the Gospel in the many languages of that day. I also am witnessing the very hearts of Jesus and Mary. I am the spouse of Mary and it was My very being that brought Jesus into Mary as a child. The fire, that you see coming from the hearts of Jesus and Mary, is the same fire of My love that ushers forth from their hearts. As I bless all of you with the fire of My love, I also bestow upon you the gifts of the Spirit. It is through My power that I speak the Gospel through your lips. This is a day to remember how much I am a part of your lives. Without My life giving Spirit you would cease to exist. I make My dwelling among you so there is a part of Jesus in every soul. That is why you must respect everyone you greet, because you are greeting Jesus and Me in those souls. Remember to constantly call on My power and strength to speak out your love of God and love of neighbor."*

Monday, May 24, 1999:

At a home Mass, after Communion, I could see Jesus offering us His cup of suffering. Jesus said: *"My people, as I stand at the altar, I offer you My cup of suffering as My apostles had to suffer as well. When I asked St. John and St. James if they were ready to drink of the cup I was about to drink, they agreed that they would. I could not promise them to be at My right hand or My left hand in Heaven, but I did promise them that they would drink from My cup of suffering. You also, I am asking if you are ready to accept My cup of suffering. Those, who say yes to believing in My Name, must accept any persecution and criticism from those who do not believe. I ask you to count the costs that you must suffer if you want to profess your love for Me. Even though you will have to suffer in this life, your suffering is not in vain. When you give your will over to Me, I will walk with you and support you on your road to Calvary. Know that whatever you will suffer, I have suffered before you. When you drink of My cup, you are also drinking of My eternal life in Heaven. Be not afraid, My children, for all that you will endure for My sake will be multiplied in the blessing of My graces among you. Those, who accept My cup, will have eternal life in My love. While those, who refuse My cup, will be lost in the eternal suffering of Hell. Rejoice in My love as I desire all of My children to be faithful to My Will."*

Later, at Adoration, I could see a glass cup raised with grapes inside. Jesus said: *"My people, you are faced in this life with a choice between taking My cup of suffering or drinking the cup of the world's pleasures. There are many who are weak in spirit and would always prefer the easy way out. These souls would rather give in to the pleasures of the flesh and drink alcohol until they are drunk instead of following My ways. I have told you many times that the road to Hell is broad, but the road to Heaven is narrow. The evil one tries to make sin look pleasurable by satisfying all of the desires of the body. But you are a spiritual person where the cravings of your soul draw you to your soul's goal of being with Me. This is your trial then that you must suffer, a struggle between the desires of the body and the desires of the soul. I call on you in your weakened state to deny the body and drink of My cup of suffering. If you give in to the cup of the world's pleasures, you will never be satisfied. Your soul can only find its peace in Me. So come, My children, and walk with Me so you can find eternal rest for your soul."*

Tuesday, May 25, 1999:

After Communion, I could see some Church pews and then a picture of the exit doors. Jesus said: *"My people, do not be in such a hurry to leave My church after Holy Communion. Many of you do not visit with Me in the Blessed Sacrament very much. So I ask you to spend a few extra moments with Me after Mass. Your schedules are always arranged for the business of your own agendas. If you could make more priorities for Me, it would be good for your soul to drink in My graces. For a short time after you receive Me in Holy Communion, you are like a Tabernacle for My Host. So spend those extra moments enjoying the graces I am blessing you with in the Sacrament of My Eucharist. Spend some time in listening to what I wish to communicate to your soul. Even come before My Tabernacle to say a few extra prayers to get you through your day. Many forget to request My help in all of your trials. By calling on Me every day, your burdens will be that much lighter. Use this extra time to thank Me for the many gifts that I have bestowed upon you. For those that spend this extra time to get closer to your Lord, you will be rewarded in knowing that you are following more of My Will than your own."*

Later, at Adoration, I could see some land with lights from a plane. There was a strong beacon of light by which an airplane was being guided to the airport. Jesus said: *"My people, I am that beacon of light by which your souls are drawn to follow Me. The airplanes travel at night and through rainy weather. They need a light and a radio beam so they can home in on where to land. Your souls crave to be with your Lord. That is why you are always searching to find Me at Mass or in My Tabernacle. My grace of love is beaming from the monstrance at adoration. You come before Me so you can find rest for your soul. A church or a chapel with the Blessed Sacrament is like a beacon of love awaiting every soul who seeks to be refreshed. You know where I am so you can direct yourselves to find Me in My Real Presence. I wish to heal all sinners. So seek Me in the priest at Confession where your sins can be forgiven. Give Me thanks that like this airport, I continue to spread My blessings of love over all of My faithful."*

Wednesday, May 26, 1999:

After Communion, I could see someone looking in a mirror. Jesus said: *"My people, you need to step back at times and see how other people view your appearance. If you are in depression or always complaining of your troubles, maybe you will find people sharing their troubles as well. However, My Gospel is one of joy and hope for the day you will share in the glory of Heaven. So put on a cheerful face and reach out to help your neighbor without all of your complaints. I am a loving God and I want all of you to show your love for others as well. Do everything to restrain your selfish interests and think more of how you can make your contribution of time and money for others. By being gracious and loving, you will be living the Gospel message and giving good example. No matter how many difficulties you will have, you should put on a happy face to show you can withstand these temptations to complain."*

Later, at Adoration, I could see a television recording as a telephone tap. Jesus said: *"My child, you will be persecuted more and more for the price of saving souls. The more places you go and the more people that hear My message to be saved through you, the more sufferings you will have to endure. Every place that you are going, is being tested by the clergy and people trying to block your visits. As people are more uncomfortable with your messages, you will endure stronger and stronger criticisms. You will only be able to travel and send your messages out for a short time. Now is the time to make the most of your visits. A time is coming when evil men will be harassing you and threatening your life. I will protect your soul, but soon you will be dearly tested for preaching in My Name. As the time of the Antichrist draws near, they will outlaw anyone openly preaching any religion but the One World religion of the Antichrist. That is why your life will be in jeopardy as evil will have its short reign. Do not fear and keep proclaiming My Name as long as you are able. I will reward all of My followers with a new life in My Era of Peace. Do not worry how these evil men will have their way, but struggle in your battle of good and evil to fight to save souls. This has been your mission from day one and it should be held up even in the face of major persecution."*

Thursday, May 27, 1999: (Mark 13:9-13, Luke 21:12-19)

After Communion, I could see a court room with a judge at the bench. Jesus said: *"My people, in the days of tribulation they will drag you to court and persecute you for believing in My Name. I will give you the strength to give witness to others in your belief in Me and by the Holy Spirit I will give you what to say in your defense. I have asked you to continue to preach in My Name to all the nations for as long as you can. Do not fear for your life, for those, who will lose their life for My sake, will save their soul. I love all of My faithful and I will come to your protection in the days of the Antichrist. Keep faithful to My Word and you will have nothing to fear. Know that when you see these things occurring, My victory is not far off."*

Later, at the prayer group, I could see someone playing on a concert piano. Jesus said: *"My people, it takes many hard hours of practice to play the piano at a concert. If just one note is off, many will notice it. You, My children, are working on your spiritual lives with the same effort. It takes much practice to bring yourself to follow My Will. I desire that you strive to be perfect also. But I am more forgiving than you are. I know that you are in a weakened state and vulnerable to sin. But I give you a way out by seeking forgiveness of your sins in Confession. Use this sacrament often so you may be brought closer to perfection."*

I could see some ships and missiles were leaving trails of smoke on their take off. Jesus said: *"My people, the wars you continue to wage are without any remorse in carrying out your selfish objectives. It is not a matter of seeking peace, but each side wants to inflict their own toll on the other side. On one side the Serbs want to rid all non-serbs from their land. The NATO side is trying to devastate the whole country in order to bring the Serb leaders to their knees. All of this destruction and killing will not solve any problems. You must pray for peace in Kosovo before this war spreads any further. Come to the peace table before it is too late."*

I could see a scene inside a small house and everything had the color green. Jesus said: *"My people, many times you desire to be rich and have no worries about having to work for a living. But life is not that easy and it does not take place the way you would want it. So you will meet many frustrations and disappointments during your life, but some of them you bring on yourselves. Expect that you will have to suffer in this life and seek My help to get you through."*

I could see a movie of a conflict between soldiers. Jesus said: *"My people, you sometimes glorify those who kill many soldiers as heroes. While it may be bravery to defend your country or your home from an aggressor, it is only accidental that you kill the other side to win. To glorify the act of killing does not give good example, especially to your children and young adults. It is the constant carnage shown on your news and in your movies that seems to glorify death in some eyes. Restrict your violence shown your children or they will think that it is normal."*

I could see a man wearing a suit and tie to Church. Jesus said: *"My people, you have become very lax in your reverence and casual in your dress even at Mass. On special occasions of weddings and funerals, you take the time and care to look presentable. Why it is when you come before your Lord at Mass, you do not see it important enough to wear your Sunday best? Even more so, your respect for My Real Presence has almost disappeared in some churches. See Me as Lord of your lives and worthy to be honored at all times."*

I could see a small boat and it was burning. Jesus said: *"My people, I have told you that if enough people do not pray to stop these wars, you will see them expand in scope. If you do not come to terms of peace, you could see this conflict increase in battles between ships. Listen to My pleas and stop trying to force your will on every country to meet your demands. You may come to regret your actions if you do not cease your hostilities."*

I could see someone descending some stairs and there was a bright light glowing that resulted. Jesus said: *"My people, I am calling on you to be peacemakers among your nations and in your families. Unless you compromise your position, there cannot be any peace. If you are really seeking My peace, you will not mind to lose face and give in to certain demands that may be required to bring about peace. It is in your selfishness of wanting your own way all of the time that causes your troubles. Look at things with love in your heart seeking to reconcile any differences you have with your neighbor. Then you will give peace a chance to succeed."*

Friday, May 28, 1999:

After Communion, I could see a large crowd in an auditorium with a bright light on the stage. Jesus said: *"My people, the harvest of souls is many, but few are the laborers to bring these souls to Me. Every soul has to answer for themselves at the judgment, because each of you has a free will. I need My faithful souls to invite and instruct these souls in My Gospel. I am asking all of My prayer warriors to redouble their efforts as the time of tribulation draws close. Pray for the conversion of poor sinners so they may change their hearts and be saved. Without someone encouraging these souls, they may never come to know Me. My Warning experience will enlighten many to change their lives. I will need many helping hands, especially family members, to guide these souls to Confession and the forgiveness of their sins. Do not act as the foolish virgins and put off your preparations for death. By being ready to receive Me now, you will love Me longer and you will not be a stranger. Those, who refuse to seek Me in love and do not seek the forgiveness of their sins, are the ones who will be cast into the eternal fire."*

Later, at Adoration, I could see a liberty bell, but it was very blurry. Jesus said: *"My people, many of your freedoms are slipping away from you very subtly. Your free speech is being eroded by interest groups. Your expression of religion is becoming more controlled through your church and state separation. Many restrictions are placed on you in the work place that even threatens your jobs. As you approach the time of the Antichrist, you will even see your money and the means to buy things become more controlled by the One World people. A time is coming when your money will be called in and only smart cards will be accepted for purchases. Once the agents of the Antichrist have control of the people in their smart cards, they will then try to force people to take these same chips in the right hand or forehead. All of this will be done to control people and force them to worship the Antichrist. Do not accept the smart cards because they have the same chip that will be placed in the hand. Those, who knowingly take the chip in the hand and worship the Antichrist, will be condemned to Hell as in My Scriptures. Awaken your people to the dangers of letting the Mark of the Beast control your lives. There will be a major crisis and unrest through wars that will enable the Antichrist to control the world. Pray to Me for protection and My angels will lead you to safety away from the influence of these evil ones. Trust and hope in My power as I will soon vanquish this evil lot and restore My peace to a new world without evil. By My help, I will protect your souls and provide for your needs."*

Saturday, May 29, 1999:

After Communion, I could see a tunnel with a light throughout it. Jesus said: *"My people, as you go through life, I am the light at the end of the tunnel. The life of a Christian is one of hope and faith in Me. I am the one you can rely on to help you through all of life's difficulties. Nothing is impossible for Me, as many things have been answered through prayer. All that is required is a steadfast love for Me and I will protect your soul from the evil one. Bear with this life for My sake and you will have eternal rest in Heaven. Your life after this life is the most important, since that is why you were created, to give glory to Me. Do not try to hang on to this life's pleasures and riches, for they are passing away tomorrow. Seek only heavenly riches, for they are everlasting. Focus your life on love of God and love of your neighbor and your life will be happy here and forever."*

Later, I could look down at night on a crowd with lights and there was a new baby. Jesus said: *"My people, I have told you that the One World people have a plan to exploit this problem with your computers at the end of the year. These people have enabled the situation by not encouraging people to fix the problem ahead of time. They even are instrumental in telling people not to worry about it. As people will flounder around in chaos, the same one world group will offer a plan to fix all of the power outages. They will then introduce a new plan for buying and selling that will utilize chips in the hand and satellites running on solar power. This is all a scheme to allow the Antichrist to have control over the earth. This will be a gradual process, but it shows you why you need to prepare both physically and spiritually for this coming trial. I will multiply the food you have stored and when they try to force the Mark of the Beast on you, I will have My angels lead you to safe havens. There again I will provide for your needs and protect you. Call on Me in your trials and I will come to your aid. Have no fear and trust in my help. As you see these things come about, know that My victory is near."*

Sunday, May 30, 1999: (Holy Trinity Sunday)

After Communion, I could see a triangle in a plane of glass which moved around in different views. Jesus said: *"My people, you are seeing I AM, the Word, and the Spirit of love representing the three Persons of the Blessed Trinity in God the Father, God the Son, and God the Holy Spirit. Wherever one of Us is present, the other two are there too, because We are inseparable. Rejoice in the graces that We pour out on mankind all over your world. We are a part of your life in the very being that you share and Our love permeates everything in creation. As you marvel at the plants, the animals, and the scenery of creation, give thanks to God for all that you have been given. The gifts of health, light, and even the air you breathe are so common to your life, you may forget that they come from God. Even the successes in your life are a result of the gifts in education and your reasoning faculties. In other words, all that you have, has come from God and do not take personal pride in the things you have been given. Love is at the core of the Blessed Trinity in the Person of the Holy Spirit. This Divine Love is a part in each soul and it is that love in you that draws you to seek your rest in Us. So come and follow the Commandments which were given to direct your love of God and love of neighbor. This mystery of the Blessed Trinity is so much a part of your life that you should recognize Us as Lord and follow the Will of God in all that you do."*

Monday, May 31, 1999: (Visitation, Memorial Day)

After Communion, I could see the curtains of a Confessional and a black tarry substance oozed out on the floor from under the curtain. Jesus said: *"My people, when you confess your sins, the priest absolves you and you become a cleansed soul as at your Baptism. When your sins are forgiven, your soul is rid of the filth of your sins. Confession lifts you up and strengthens you with sanctifying grace. Confession is a haven for sinners, because it takes you from the grasp of the evil one, and puts you into the safety of My protective arms. Do not wallow in your sins and let despair and depression rule your life. Seek Me in the priest so I can loose the bonds of sin that control you. Once you have been freed of your sins, you become a new creation and vibrant with My life within you. No longer will the guilt of your sin weigh you down, but your joy will be complete in My love. So do not put off going to Confession because of your fear of the priest. It is the evil one who encourages your spiritual laziness. Wake up out of your weakness in sin and move into My light by confessing your sins to the priest. Rejoice that you have My sacrament of Reconciliation available at your nearest church."*

Later, at Adoration, I could see an icon of the Infant Jesus and then a rocking chair in motion. Mary said: *"My dear children, you need to imitate me in helping your neighbor as I helped Elizabeth. It was spontaneous from the moment the angel told me of Elizabeth's pregnancy, that I would go and help her as soon as possible. Look for these moments of opportunity to reach out and help your neighbor spontaneously without concern for your own inconvenience. It is the intention of your heart that Jesus considers in every one of your actions. Sometimes it is easy for you to offer help. Other times it may require you to go the extra mile to help someone. It is for these extra efforts that you will earn your reward, since these efforts take more self-giving of a person than a casual helping. Jesus gave you the story of the good Samaritan as an example of how to treat your neighbor. So think with your heart and your love will show forth in your actions."*

Tuesday, June 1, 1999:

After Communion, I could see some rows of wheat next to a stream. Jesus said: *"My people, you need to be always ready to die, because you are only here for a season. See that the harvest of wheat is about to be taken where the wheat will be gathered into My barn, while the tares will be burned in the fire. The stream is to indicate how your sins have been washed away and now you can drink and take your rest. All those, who have been faithful to Me in life, will have their reward waiting for them in Heaven. Follow My Will so you can yield thirty, sixty, and a hundredfold."*

Later, at Adoration, I could see an assembly line where computers and monitors were being put together. Jesus said: *"My people, I am showing you how much your technology has advanced in a short time. But man has become puffed up in his pride in what he thinks he can control. Many of your machines and programs are not always compatible with each other. If you have difficulties now with all of your upgrades, how are you to handle the additional problems in reading 2000? In addition to your computer problems, you will be fortunate to even have power to debug them. Man has been so confident in himself, that he cannot believe there is a problem that he cannot solve. Since you have relied more on yourselves than on Me, it will be your own imperfections that will destroy your technology. There will be some in power who will try to take advantage of the coming breakdowns in your society. There will be many hardships and shortages as a result of these problems. That is why I have asked you to prepare both spiritually and physically. Have many blessed sacramentals, go to frequent Confession, and develop a strong prayer life. In your homes you could set aside some extra food, water and fuel for your friends and relatives. I will multiply what you need, but it is your responsibility to be prudent and discern your individual needs. The coming tribulation will be a test of your faith. Remember to call on My help and that of your guardian angels when the evil lot will take control of the worldly things. Fear not as I will come to release your bonds."*

Wednesday, June 2, 1999:

After Communion, I could see an up close scene of a wedding ring. Jesus said: *"My people, the love between a man and a woman is the example of My love for you when I called My Church as the bride and Myself as the groom. Those married in My Church experience the graces I bestow upon them in the Sacrament of Matrimony. There are many forces working against the family in your modern world that even challenges marriage as an institution. Man in his greed for things and pleasures has brought about many divorces, same sex marriages, and couples living together without marriage. The respect for the marriage bond has been cheapened by your pornography and the search for money in your adulterous movies and TV programs. Those, who have committed their lives to each other, should work at their marriages to keep them together. You need to show your love for each other every day, even in the little things you do. Communicating your love verbally is needed in marriage as much as your love for Me should come in your daily prayers. Love can soothe many of your problems, but it requires a commitment from each of the spouses. I love each of you so much, and I ask you to accept Me as a partner in your marriages. When there is faith in each spouse, those marriages are the ones that endure. So pray for the success of your marriages and do not treat these unions lightly. This love between a husband and wife is to be treasured and held in your esteem as the model for life as was given in My Holy Family."*

Later, at Adoration, I could see God the Father in the sky and then a silhouette of the tablets of the Ten Commandments. God the Father said: *"I AM is showing you how history will be repeated. In the days of Moses you witnessed in the Scriptures how I protected My people from the Egyptian army. I nurtured My people in the desert with manna and water. While I was giving the Ten Commandments to Moses, the people became restless and they fashioned a golden calf to worship. I gave these Commandments for all of mankind so you would be able to show your love for God and your love for your neighbor. My wrath rose up and I was about to punish those worshiping this false idol. But Moses spared My hand of the punishment I was about to deal My people. This is where the people of your age are repeating the errors of the past, because you are worshiping the false idols of the world instead of Me. You will see an age of tribulation come both as a punishment for your sins and a test of your faith in believing in My Son, Jesus. My Son will assemble the angels of Heaven and they will do battle with the evil spirits and the evil people. Jesus will bring His triumph against Satan and the Antichrist, and they will be chained in Hell. Then you will be raised above the earth as I will recreate the earth into a paradise without evil. Then My Son will bring His faithful down to the earth to enjoy an age of peace as in Adam's day. You all will then grow in perfection so you will be ready when I will receive you into Heaven on your resurrection on the last day."*

Thursday, June 3, 1999:

After Communion, I could see a dump truck carrying away a load of dirt. Jesus said: *"My people, just as this dump truck, I come around to all of your souls so you can load the filth of your sins on Me. As you have your sins forgiven, I have to bear the load for all of mankind. Just as you dump your refuse outside the city, they took Me outside of Jerusalem to crucify Me. It was on the cross that I took on all of your sins and made an offering of My life up to My Father. This Divine Sacrifice of My life was the payment for all of your sins in the past, present and the future. You are still weak in your sins, but you need to cleanse them from your soul through Confession. That is why I continue to come among you in mercy seeking to cure your souls and carry away all of your burdens of guilt. Reach out to Me in Confession and be healed of all of your afflictions of this world."*

Later, at the prayer group, I could see some missiles taking off. Jesus said: *"My people, several nations have been testing their missiles so they could claim to deliver nuclear weapons. This is not to be taken lightly that such technology is being pro-liferated among your eastern nations. Instead, it means My faith-ful need to be praying more than even that such weapons are never used. Small conflicts between nations and the availability of these weapons could lead to their use if these nations were threatened with takeover."*

I could see a large crowd watching some UN proceedings. Jesus said: *"My people, you have seen some signs in Kosovo of a pos-sible peace agreement. If the leaders are allowed to save face, a compromise could be reached. But if either side is adamant to their own demands, you could see a continuation of this conflict. Pray that your leaders will come to a reasonable compromise without violations of either side. The longer this conflict contin-ues, the greater the chance of this war's expansion."*

I could see a farmer storing his grain after the harvest. Jesus said: *"My people, beware of the people who are in control of the buying and selling of your food. Many of your farmers are being threatened with bankruptcy because of artificially low prices. But once the food is passed on to the consumer, your prices rise dra-matically. Pray for fairness in this supply and demand or those manipulating the prices could bring on major food shortages. Your food has still been at risk to your weather. Storing some extra food may be necessary if you will experience any problems in transporting the food to your stores."*

I could see some cars for mining ore on some tracks. Jesus said: *"My people, many of your industrial factories are changing in the makeup of their workers. More of your corporations are merging to bigger companies which places more power in fewer hands. These mergers threaten your workers and have reduced competition. Your prosperous economy could start cracking when fewer are making adequate salaries. Turn your lives away from greedy profits or the poor will continue to increase."*

I could see a large structure that was protecting a farmer's crops. Jesus said: *"My people, as extremes continue to occur in droughts and floods, you may have to start sheltering your fields from the heat and the cold. Your available water and the storms, that you are seeing, will be having a disastrous effect on your crops. You will have to be more and more industrious in growing your food as it becomes scarce for some. Soon your survival will be more of a concern than your previous concerns with your leisure time."*

I could see some Middle Eastern people in turbans. Jesus said: *"My people, you are seeing dramatic changes in the heads of state in the Middle-East. If there are no improvements in the peace in this area, you could see another hotbed of unrest in this area. Continue to pray for peace all over the world, since there are many conflicts going on at any one time. It is greed and power that are at the root of these conflicts. Pray for more peace-makers to be effective in bringing these warring countries to the peace table. Restrain your fighting which only promotes destruc-tion and killing."*

I could see some people building a home in the hills in the wilderness. Jesus said: *"My people, there are some people building refuges in the hills because they are fearful of the coming tribulation. While some have discerned this by prayer, this is not possible for many of lesser means. You are seeing a battle of good and evil where you will be facing principalities and powers. So ask for My help in bringing you through this time which will be a test of evil that you have yet to see."*

Friday, June 4, 1999:

After Communion, I could see a house in a town and then a woman in a wedding dress. Jesus said: *"My people, you are seeing a woman representing Sara, the one who lost seven husbands to the devil, Asmodeus. On hearing the prayer of Sara and Tobias, I sent My angel St. Raphael to guide and protect them. Both Sara and Tobias prayed before their wedding night that God would protect Tobias from the demon. This prayer is an example that all couples should pray for their own marriages. St. Raphael restrained the demon as Tobias received Sara as his wife. The prayers of Tobias and Sara were answered through My angel. You have your own guardian angels that you can call on for help through Me. They are always at your side to guide you. Give glory to God that I have seen fit to have each of you watched over by one of My angels."*

Later, at St. John's Adoration, Danvers, Mass., I could look up at a ceiling and there was a circle of images that were rotating so much that it was making me dizzy. Jesus said: *"My people, I am not giving you the date of the warning, but only to tell you that it is close. The warning will be an extension of My mercy, but not something to fear. Those, who do not have their souls prepared to meet Me, could experience a traumatic event. I am speaking of those souls in mortal sin and those immersed so much in the world that they have lost their faith. For when you see yourself through My eyes, you will see how much your sins offend Me. It will be the overbearing guilt of your sin that will disturb many the most. That is why you would be better to go to frequent Confession so your soul would be constantly cleansed with My forgiveness and My grace. By being properly disposed in your soul beforehand, you will enjoy My favor of mercy when you are faced with this Warning experience. I have told you in My Gospels to be ever watchful when I would return. By your spiritual readiness to greet Me, you will be more disposed to the things of Heaven than those of the earth. I recommend that you pray for your soul to be saved and to pray for the conversion of sinners who could be turned around by My mercy of a second chance. After the Warning, this will be the time when your prayers for your friends and relatives will be most effective. So call on My help and the saints and angels to bring as many souls to conversion as you can, especially after the Warning. I will be granting this mercy as a last chance for many souls to be converted. Do not give up on souls refusing My love, but be persistent in your prayers to their dying days."*

Saturday, June 5, 1999:

At St. Mary's Church, Danvers, Mass., after Communion, I could see a small Church and then another scene where the flags of many nations were displayed. Jesus said: *"My people, today's reading speaks about the widow's mite in that she gave of her substance to the temple. This is a strong lesson in alms giving that everyone is liable for the support of My Church. There are some who tithe of their income in giving of their substance and time for the poor and My Church. It is by your own free will how much you wish to donate to charity and My Church, but I give you this challenge to share as much as you can and not to be selfish. Your money here is very elusive, but whatever you give will be stored in Heaven. I challenged the rich man to be perfect by giving all that he had to the poor and follow Me. In the same way I challenge every soul to share not only their money, but to give your whole life over to My Will. You have been given a gift of life and many other blessings. You can return your love to Me by your gift of self in following My ways. You are torn to choose between heaven and earth. Choose Me first and everything will be given you. Those, who share with others in their time and money will receive My reward both here and in Heaven. So be open to My call and help those in need and you will have My joy and peace in all that you do. It is better to give than receive. The more you share with others the more your love is seen by Me and your neighbor."*

Later, at St. Mary's Church, Rowley, Mass., I could see a Host blurry at first and then clear in a monstrance. Jesus said: *"My people, I have promised you that I would be with you to the end of this age. See that I am always with you in My Real Presence of the Eucharist. I am the Bread of life and those, who eat of My Body and drink My Blood, will have eternal life with Me. It is a mystery to your senses how the God of your life can be wholly present in the Consecrated Host. Each Mass is a gift of the Transubstantiation of the bread to My Body and Blood. This miracle of My Real Presence is the core of your faith in Me. As you receive Me in Holy Communion, you can witness My love in your soul and the grace of this sacrament. This spiritual nourishment is necessary for your soul as I give you My rest and peace. You search the earth to be satisfied, but you can never find rest in your soul from earthly things. Your soul craves to be with Me in Heaven. Your receiving Me in Holy Communion is the closest piece of Heaven that your soul can share in this life. So give Me praise and thanks for this gift of Myself to your soul. Today, you see Me with the eyes of faith. In Heaven you will witness Me in My beatific vision, and you will be completely wrapped in My being in your perfection. In Heaven after the final judgment you will be spiritually whole with your glorified body and your white washed robes. You will sing your praise of Me in harmony with the Communion of Saints and the angels."*

Sunday, June 6, 1999: (Corpus Christi)

At St. Basil's Church, Methuen, Mass., after Communion, I could see Jesus breaking the bread. Jesus said: *"My people, My disciples recognized Me on the road to Emmaus at the breaking of the bread. I have given you the bread of life through My death on the cross. When you gather at My Eucharist to share My Body at the Mass, you are all joined in the larger Mystical Body of My Church. The bread I multiplied for the 4,000 and the 5,000 is a bread that was temporary and lasted for one meal. The Consecrated Host, that I share with you, is the bread of the soul that will last forever. At every Mass you renew this spiritual life within you with My Real Presence in the Host. Guard your souls from the evil one's temptations through Confession so you will be always ready to receive Me in Holy Communion. Even My angels have Me in their presence, but not in this intimate contact as you receive Me. So rejoice in your praise of My glory and be thankful for this gift of Myself to you. Do not become complacent in receiving Me, but always appreciate the sacredness of My Presence by your constant reverence. By kneeling and receiving Me on the tongue, you can give witness to the glory of My Presence. I love you, My people, and My coming down to you in this bread is an example of how much I long to be with you, whenever you can receive Me or visit Me in My Tabernacle. I long for the day when I can bring all of My faithful to Heaven. Then you will be in awe of My Presence face to face and you will no longer need My Sacramental Presence."*

Monday, June 7, 1999:

After Communion, I could see a stone wall and in front was a small monstrance with a small Host inside. Jesus said: *"My people, during the time of tribulation, you will need to preserve and protect My Sacred Hosts from desecration. I have asked you to store monstrances or reliquaries for the time of schism in My Church. There will be only a few priests available for Mass, so it will be hard to locate a Mass. It is during the time of a religious persecution that it will be hard to locate My Hosts. Many of your churches will be burned and desecrated by evil people. This is why it will be permitted to have My Hosts protected at that time. This presence of Mine will be an uplift to those faithful who cannot get to a Mass. You can also call on Me for spiritual communion and I will have My angels place My sacred Hosts on your tongue. I have promised you that I would be with you to the end of this age, and I will be with you through My Real Presence in My Hosts."*

Later, at Adoration, I could see a sign of nuclear power in the darkness. This sign was the model of a large nucleus with electrons passing around the nucleus. Jesus said: *"My people, I am showing you this symbol of an atom to point out to you how dangerous your nuclear weapons are. You can remember how many thousands of people were killed when two cities in Japan were bombed. Many of your modern day nuclear bombs have more destructive power than these early weapons. Because of this potential, even more lives are in peril with the large numbers of bombs already loaded on your missiles and submarines. There are many problems in keeping these weapons away from terrorists. A new threat is the potential problem with your computer controls and electrical circuits that could launch these weapons accidentally. Pray, My children, with enough fervor that these weapons will not be launched. If there is not enough prayer for peace, you could see several nations annihilated as foretold at Fatima. See with so many conflicts going on in the world that such an accident or an intentional act could cause such destruction. You need to persist in your prayers more than ever."*

Tuesday, June 8, 1999:

After Communion, I could see a gutter and the water running down the pipe. Jesus said: *"My people, as I talked to My people in Israel of salt and lamp stands, today I am showing you this rain gutter for disposal of the water. There are many things you dispose in the trash bin, but if it was not taken away, it would inundate you and possibly cause disease. In the same way in the body if you did not flush away the toxins in your blood, you could be poisoned and die. This is true of your soul as well. Over time you accumulate the filth of your sins which need to be cleansed or you will suffocate and die from your sins. Death to the soul is more important than death to the body. The soul goes on for eternity and if you become lost in sin, you could spend forever in Hell on your judgment. So it is necessary that you get to Confession often to cleanse your souls. You cleanse the body and remove the trash. What better need do you have in cleansing your soul from sin?"*

Later, at Adoration, I could see a woman coming to Mass in an inappropriate length dress. Jesus said: *"My people, I am asking you again to come to Mass on Sunday appropriately dressed. It is summer and once it is hot, some become too lax in their dress. Most of your modern churches are cooled and do not require scanty clothing. When you come to give glory to your Lord, you are not going to the beach. So do not wear scanty clothing and shorts to church. Take a lesson from your European churches that do not allow shorts and immodest dress. With such clothing you may give scandal or cause sin in others. Give respect to Me in your clothing and you could wear your better clothes to show Me your reverence. You come to Mass to receive Me in Holy Communion, so come in a proper frame of mind for prayer and worship. I love you for coming to church, but I ask you to give good example in your dress."*

Wednesday, June 9, 1999:

After Communion, I could see some bare shelves at the grocery stores. Jesus said: *"My people, I am calling you to prepare for the coming disasters and shortages that will be affecting your food supplies. Your weather patterns are changing and they will cause major problems in growing your crops. In the past you have been spared because you could buy crops from other places in the world. In the future these alternate sources will have the same problems that you have with droughts, fires, floods, and high wind storms. Because your food will be in short supply from weather and computer related problems, now is the time to stock up your own food storage. This is not hoarding, but to be prudent in providing for your friends and relatives who are not saving their own food. As food is cleared from your stores because of transportation and stock flow problems, there will be major problems as people will be searching to find food. Riots will break out and the military may have to be deployed when martial law could be declared. You need to prepare spiritually as well in your daily prayers. With My help I will guide you through these difficult times and I will even multiply what you need. So have no fear."*

Later, at Adoration, I could see a television screen and there were numbers flashing across the screen. Then the Antichrist appeared on the TV. Jesus said: *"My people, I have given you advice in not to watch your TVs, especially after the Warning, because the Antichrist will use this means to control people. Once the Antichrist appears on TV, he will have the image of the Beast viewed on every TV all over the world. He will have demonic powers and he will control people's minds by suggestion, his charisma and the means to send subliminal messages that attempt to force people to worship him. Because of this evil influence of the Antichrist, do not even view him or his picture. For anyone claiming to be Me or greater than Me, do not listen to them nor hold any of his pictures or literature. These things will take on an evil nature of their own and they will cause evil or strange things to occur if you keep them in your home. Call on My help through prayer and your blessed sacramentals to protect you from any evil during the tribulation. I am warning you not to look on the image of the beast, not to take his Mark, and not to worship him. I am the one true God and I alone am worthy of your worship. I will send you My angels to guide you and protect you. Without My help, your soul will be lost in these evil days. Pray to keep faithful and you will see My victory and your reward on earth and in Heaven."*

Thursday, June 10, 1999:

After Communion, I could see some large indirect lighting in the sky that I sensed was brought on by the Antichrist. Jesus said: *"My people, the coming Antichrist will have demonic powers such that he will call on special lights from the sky. He will use illusions and magic to simulate great lights in the sky as an aurora borealis. In actuality he will be using reflective satellites to cause these seeming miracles. These things will be permitted for him to test the faith of My followers. Do not worship this evil one who will claim to be Me and do not be misled by any appearing miracles. Do not take the Mark of the Beast to buy and sell, but only worship Me. I will come in wonder on a cloud and everyone will know of My coming. So do not be taken in by this great deceiver who will try to persuade even My elect to follow him. I will be by your side at all times. So call on My help and I will protect your soul throughout the whole tribulation. Avoid the influence of the Antichrist and do not believe this man of lies."*

Later, at the prayer group, I could see some men working on making fast cars. Jesus said: *"My people, you have spent many hours working on various means of transportation. If your fuel supplies become unavailable, you will have to go back to your early means of travel. Your computer failures could effect your lifestyles drastically and return you to a farming society instead of so much manufacturing. A slower paced life would cause some problems to adjust, but would be better for you. It is those who will take advantage of the coming turmoil that may allow the Antichrist to take over. This tribulation is not far off. So you should make your spiritual and physical preparations."*

I could see some trees next to a military base. Jesus said: *"My people, as you look at the coming occupation forces of Kosovo, you could be seeing what happens in the chaos of war. With coming food shortages and fuel shortages, you too could see chaos that would bring on a state of martial law. A police state is already planned for your country should your year end problems be serious and lengthy to fix. You would be prudent to stock fuel, water and food for your next winter. I will be with you in prayer, but your action could lessen the severity of your shortages."*

I could see some larger platters for making computer chips. Jesus said: *"My people, your technology has advanced so fast, that you have not planned for any failures in your equipment. You have been content to replace older computer chips with more powerful ones, but the built in flaws in your hardware and software have been intentionally overlooked. Those in control of your society have known about your date problems, but they have not planned enough to fix it on purpose. This is the means by which the Antichrist will be given his chance to rebuild a controlled people. Pray to Me and your angels to lead you to safe places away from the evil plotting of men."*

I could see a marble stairway up a hill outside. Jesus said: *"My people, to have a good spiritual life you must struggle in an uphill battle. Each day you need to be advancing in your holiness on your way to perfection. This will require you to put aside the desires of the flesh and focus on imitating My life. Living a holy life is possible, but it means giving over your will to following My Will. Continue to work on your path to Heaven because it is a life long task."*

I could see a very modern black car. Jesus said: *"My people, as you strive in the world to move ahead in your possessions, you will be shocked when your whole lifestyle is thrown into disarray. I have told you many times that because of your sins, you would be stripped of your possessions. As your power shortages become evident, you will be frustrated when many of your electrical toys fail to work. You will soon see how vulnerable you have been all along. So prepare now to face a different lifestyle without all of your comforts. When these things take place, you will be dependent on My multiplying your food and feeding you My heavenly bread. Rejoice, because My victory and a new Era of Peace are coming soon."*

I could see many question marks as people will be in confusion wanting to know what to do. Jesus said: *"My people, through all of the coming tribulation, there is no reason to be fearful when I will be with you. You will be tested by an evil you have yet to see, but think of the miraculous ways I protected My people in the desert. You will be witnessing a modern day Exodus where you will be depending on My providing you water, food, and shelter. Do not depend on the evil ones to help you, for they will give you anything to buy your soul. Do not let the evil one control you with the Mark of the Beast. Refuse to worship him and refuse his jobs and food. Your soul is too valuable to give up. With trust and hope in Me I will help you to endure this trial. Keep your faith in Me and you will have nothing to fear."*

I could see a beautiful sunset and the earth during the Era of Peace. Jesus said: *"My people, I am showing you the glorious heaven on earth that awaits those that will remain faithful to Me. To suffer for a short time is well worth the reward that awaits you in this paradise. A world of love and peace will sweep in after My victory over the Antichrist. You may suffer your purgatory on earth, but I give you hope in promising you a better tomorrow. Those, who give in to the evil one, will suffer a living hell on earth and below. Those, who refuse the Antichrist, will have everything to live for."*

Friday, June 11, 1999: (Sacred Heart of Jesus)

After Communion, I could see a heart and then Jesus with a shepherd's staff. Jesus said: *"My people, this feast day of My Sacred Heart focuses on My love for all of mankind. My Heart has been bruised by your sins and insults and even pierced when I was already dead. On the cross I gave every drop of blood up to redeem all of you. This sacrifice of My life is the most perfect act of love that God could perform for all of humanity. This was the plan of God once it was promised that a redeemer would come to save all peoples. Your world is an example of the struggles going on between the forces of good and evil. The evidence of hate and evil is all around you in the wars and killings going on in your abortions. Even though evil abounds, I give you hope in the power of My Real Presence in the world. I am also searching for the return of your love for Me. I created each of you for the glory of God and to share My love with you. I have given each life a plan and a purpose for your being here in helping others. Share your love with Me by preserving all life that you encounter. Pray to have your love remain faithful to Me and continue to follow My Will. By working in harmony with Me, that is your best means to show your love for Me. I am in essence asking you to join your heart with Mine in living out your faith."*

Later, at the Rosary group, I could see people coming to pray as they were walking down a hill. Jesus said: *"My dear people, I am grateful for all of My faithful who gather together in My Name. On My feast day of My Sacred Heart I pour out My heavenly graces on all here present. You are all joined in sharing the love of My Sacred Heart. My love burns in all of your hearts as you share your love with Me. I love you all so much and your faithfulness warms My heart with your tender devotions in prayer. Continue to gather regularly in your prayers, so you will be strengthened to endure your trials of today and your tribulation of tomorrow. You all are special to Me and My protection overshadows all of your work. Continue to pray for My intentions and those of My mother so you may have peace and love spread all over the world."*

Saturday, June 12, 1999: (The Immaculate Heart of Mary)

After Communion, I could see Mary standing in white and then she was standing in darkness. Mary said: *"My dear children, I am happy to come and comfort you as a mother. My heavenly heart is open to share my love with you and I am constantly sharing my heart with Jesus. My presence with you in messages and apparitions is about to come to an end. This is why I am appearing in the darkness. I have been heralding the second coming of my Son and soon after a brief tribulation, you will see our triumph over Satan and the Antichrist. Do not be sad about not having me visit you, for this is but another sign of the End Times. Rejoice as you see the start of the tribulation, for you know my Son's victory is not far off. I will still be protecting you with my mantle, even during the tribulation. Have confidence in Heaven's help as you will soon see the last battle of good and evil."*

Later, I could see some stone grottos of water. Jesus said: *"My people, My mother has assumed the role of announcing My coming again. She is very much like St. John the Baptist before My first coming. She also will be decreasing in giving messages, as I will be increasing the messages given to My people. Mary is still your mother and she will still spread her mantle of protection among her children at the refuges during the tribulation. It will be her grottos of water that will provide you both water to drink and healing waters for the sick. So do not be disheartened in her decreased appearances, but know that it is her intention to help and lead you safely into this coming tribulation."*

Sunday, June 13, 1999:

After Communion, I could see an open window to let fresh air in. Jesus said: *"My people, you open windows in your houses to let the fresh air in. At times your souls get stuffed up with your sins. By going to Confession frequently, you can cleanse your sins through My forgiveness. Part of your problem with your sins is that you need to put more of My love into your hearts. When your hearts are cold, please open your hearts to let Me come into your lives and warm your hearts with My love. Once you take away your self love and your own agendas and replace it with My love and My Will, you will find everyone more open to love you. You need to recognize when love is missing. That is what creates greed and wars. Hate and unrest are the influence of the evil one. Satan will not lead you to Me but only to worldly cares. If you seek My love, you will find peace and rest in My arms. I love you unconditionally and My heart is always open to receive you. When you follow My peace plan to love God and love your neighbor as yourself, then love will come into your world. You have to desire love by your own free will to make it happen."*

Monday, June 14, 1999: (Mass for St. Anthony of Padua)

After Communion, I could see a large empty cross and then St. Anthony appeared in his brown robes in place of the cross. St. Anthony said: *"My dear children, many pilgrims have come to Padua to give me thanks for prayers answered. Even some have found what they were not looking for, and that is the peace of Jesus. It is very true that those, who find Jesus in their lives, have discovered the richest of treasures that they could find. It is truly better to be rich in your spiritual life than to gain the whole world in your earthly life. I am amused how some people have their faith renewed in finding the littlest of earthly things. I have shared with you before that it would be better for people to petition for heavenly gifts than your simple earthly things that are gone tomorrow. I will admit that I still love to be challenged in faith even over the little things in your lives. Even more so as Jesus said, if you ask for even miraculous things in His Name, he would grant your request if you had the faith of a mustard seed."*

Later, at Adoration, I could see an old grandfather sitting on a chair. All around him were the drawings of grammar school children in the lower grades. Jesus said: *"My people, I am showing you, America, the signs of a missing generation between the grandparents and the grandchildren of today. During the last twenty years, you are missing part of your population from your abortions and low family planning. If you did not have so much immigration from refugees and other countries, you would have even less population. Your family traditions have been so eroded that you now only have a third of your households as traditional families. You have many divorced and single parent families as well as unmarried couples. This has taken a toll on the morals of your children and your adults. Your salaries will be diminishing because of less manufacturing and poorly educated children. Your older generation will have to depend on themselves more in the future. What you are seeing is the demise of America because you have lost your love of Me. It is not too late to turn your country back to Me, but you will require a re-education of proper morals and following My Commandments. When you love yourselves more than your creator, My blessings will be taken away. That is why you have had to suffer the losses you have seen in your possessions from many kinds of disasters. Now is the time for America to turn back to Me in prayer, seeking the forgiveness of your sins. When you stop your abortions and your sins of the flesh, then your blessings will return. If you do not face the fact of your decadence, your ruination will begin soon."*

Tuesday, June 15, 1999:

After Communion, I could see from behind the cross of Jesus all of the people at church. Light was shining through a large stained glass window in the back of the church. Jesus said: *"My people, in today's Gospel I have asked you to love your enemies and pray for your persecutors. This message of love is one that goes beyond most people's comfort zone because it makes you vulnerable with no defense. My children, if you are proclaiming My love, do not make excuses to accommodate those who may be offended by My Words. If you take a stand for life and reach out in love to preserve life, continue to live My Gospel without worrying about the consequences. In your mission to bring souls to Me in the forgiveness of Confession, continue your struggle against the evil powers of Satan. As I ask you to seek perfection, do not be afraid to accept criticism and reach out in love to accept even your persecutors. When you love your neighbor, you are not to make exceptions. When you proclaim My Gospel, you cannot be hypocrites. This will call you to make hard choices in defending life in the womb and even in the prisons. This love of mine calls you to stop your wars for whatever reasons you have. Pray that you will have the strength to live what you believe."*

Later, at Adoration, I could see a farmer's hat and a shaft of wheat in front of it. Jesus said: *"My people, I am showing you the wheat and the tares that will be separated when I come again. As I told you in My Gospel, I am allowing the good and the bad to live together because if I uprooted the weeds, I may uproot the wheat as well. My love shines on the good and the bad souls, as I love all of you. The evil ones are being given their free will so they could still change their ways. My faithful must put up with evil around them, yet your good example may bring souls to love Me. When the tribulation comes, My faithful will need My strength for protection. Those, who are still evil, will be sifted by*

Satan. I will not test you beyond your endurance, so this time of purification will not last long. When I come in judgment, I will purify the earth of all evil. It is then that the evil ones will pay for their sins. These evil ones will be separated from My faithful and the evil ones will suffer a living hell on earth and an eternal pain in Hell itself. My faithful I will raise up as I will renew the earth, and you will experience Heaven on earth in My Era of Peace. Have no fear, for your reward will be great both on earth and in Heaven."

Wednesday, June 16, 1999:

After Communion, I could see people in the pews at church and a large black shadow come over them. Jesus said: *"My people, I am warning you again about the coming of an evil Masonic Antipope who will try and mislead even My elect.... Keep faithful To My Commandments and pray for strength in these end days, as My remnant church will have to go underground to avoid persecution and being misled. A schism will occur in My Church where each person will have to decide to either follow Me or the evil Antipope.... Call on Me and I will have your guardian angel lead you to a safe refuge. Have trust and faith that I will protect your soul during this tribulation. Continue to strengthen your prayer life so you will be able with My help to endure this trial."*

Later, at Adoration, I could see mirrors in a beautiful dressing room. Jesus said: *"My people of America, you have been spoiled with your freedoms and affluence. Because you have not seen persecutions and have had everything you needed, you have become complacent in your worldly things. Even some have depended more on themselves than on Me. You have had many blessings over the years, yet because of your unrepentant attitude about your sins, you will see these blessings dissipate. It is your spiritual laziness that can be the most danger to your souls. Some have even made gods out of their desires for fame, money, and sports. Focus your attention on loving Me and pleasing Me in prayer. It is the desire for a purified and perfected spiritual life that My love draws you to have eternal life. You will soon be tested by an evil persecution that you have yet to see. Do not take the Mark of the Beast or give any allegiance to the Antichrist. This tribulation will test My faithful dearly, but do not give up and trust in My help. So pray much, while you have the time, to strengthen your resolve to fight Satan and all of his evil ones who will be seeking to destroy you."*

Thursday, June 17, 1999:

After Communion, I could see a huge tsunami wave of water coming ashore from an earthquake at sea. Jesus said: *"My people, this wave of water, I am showing you, is a sign of the increasing earthquakes you will be seeing as the End Times become more apparent. The recent earthquakes in Columbia and Mexico are on the western plate that has the most activity on your continent. The other signs of pestilence and famine will become more widespread with your weather changes and your computer problems. Radiation from the sun will cause more problems at the sun spot peak year because of your increased amount of satellites and the less protection from your ozone layers. All of these events, taken as a whole, should emphasize to you that the time of your tribulation is near. The good news is that My triumph is very close as well. You will be tried for a brief time, but My faithful should look forward to sharing in My Era of Peace, which will come after I purify the earth and recreate paradise once again. Have faith and trust in Me that the evil men and evil spirits will not be on the earth much longer. Those souls, who do not convert their lives even after the Warning, are the souls who will be banished from My Kingdom to an eternity in Hell. Think twice in what you will do, because after your decision, there will be no turning back."*

Later, at the prayer group, I could see an angel adoring Jesus in the monstrance. I asked Jesus for permission for my angel Mark to speak. He said: *"My dear little ones, do not be afraid of the coming End Times. Jesus has assigned an angel to be at each one's side. Those, who remain faithful to Jesus, have nothing to fear. You may be tested with persecution and some may even be martyred for the name of Jesus. But your souls will be protected from all of the demons. I have come to give you comfort that we will be guarding your souls for Jesus and leading you to His refuges."*

I could see some spring flowers and a crown of thorns was raised among them. Jesus said: *"My people, when you see the trees budding and the first flowers coming up, you know spring is coming. Even so, as you see the signs in the sky and evil reaching new heights, you know it is a sign of the coming tribulation. You will suffer a purgatory for your sins on earth, since everyone must endure their Calvary. Then soon you will see My triumph as I cast the evil ones into Hell and I will raise up My faithful in a new paradise on earth. Your birth pangs must be suffered before you can share in My glory.*"

I could see balloons and an unusual celebration at Mass on the altar. Jesus said: "*My people, there are some who abuse the reverence that should be conducted during the Mass. If you really love Me, you would follow My traditions and not stage unnecessary dramatics at the Mass. I have given you every good gift and even My life on the cross. Show Me your love and respect by being reverent at My Masses.*"

I could see some horses and a rider dressed in black representing death as he was riding toward me. Jesus said: "*My people, your time is running out until the time of the Apocalypse will be upon you. The scene of the black horseman is the sign of death and plagues that will afflict you during the tribulation. I have encouraged you to prepare spiritually for this time by frequent Confession. You need to have your souls ready to receive Me as the wise virgins. Do not wait until it is too late and you let Satan take your soul. Act now for now is the acceptable time for salvation.*"

I could see some white bread spread all over a crowd. Jesus said: "*My people, have no fear of what you shall eat or what you will wear. My heavenly Father fed those in the desert with the manna. You are so valuable to Me that I will not let you starve in the tribulation. I will give you My manna once again and your food will be multiplied for all that you need. Have faith in My promises and you will receive a heavenly reward. You may be tested in this life, but you will rejoice in the peace and glory of your next life.*"

I could see a building honoring President Lincoln and then his statue. Jesus said: "*My people, if you can honor your great ones with such beautiful monuments, how much more should you honor Me at Sunday Mass. I died for your sins and I suf-*

fered much to bring you salvation. Give thanks and glory to Me in all that you do every day. I love you so much and I ask you to love Me in return. Give in to following My Will and everything will be given you."

I could see a large circle with a computer inside and a diagonal red line drawn across the circle. Jesus said: *"My people, this picture is a symbol to you that your computers will not be working much longer. Man has been so proud of his accomplishments, but now all of your society will come crashing down with the year two thousand problem. Many have proposed ways to fix this problem, but your leaders would have none of it. You are dealing with a planned destruction of modern life as you know it. Prepare to face a very mundane lifestyle in your next year. The One World people are planning your demise. They will then bring forth the Mark of the Beast to control the people. Do not be influenced by evil's solutions. Depend on what I have asked you to prepare and with My help you will succeed in saving your souls."*

Friday, June 18, 1999:

After Communion, I could see a vertical tunnel with a pole as for a fireman. Jesus said: *"My people, a day is coming when you will have to leave your house in haste as the day of tribulation arrives. In the days of the Exodus they ate unleavened bread and bitter herbs as in a meal of haste to leave. So it will be in your modern day Exodus when My faithful will be in haste to save their lives. When you see ... the agents of the Antichrist placing the Mark of the Beast on people; and when people will be in chaos from looting and killing for food, this will be the time to go into hiding. Call on Me and I will have your guardian angels lead you to a place of holy ground or a cave, which ever is closer. I will protect the souls of My faithful from any evil that you will face. There will be some who will be caught that may face martyrdom. Your faith is your most precious gift to protect. Even if people threaten you with death for My Name's sake, never give in to worshiping anyone else but Me. Never accept the Mark of the Beast, no matter how much they will promise you, and never worship the Antichrist. When your jobs, money or other lives are even at stake, do not give in to anyone's demands. You would rather die as a martyr than be cast into Hell for eternity. You will be faced with a battle of good and evil that you have yet to see. Pray for My grace and strength to withstand all of your trials. You will suffer a brief time, but your reward for your faithfulness will be beyond your dreams. I have repeated this message many times, but it is important to repeat it for those who may think taking the Mark will get them out of suffering. I assure you, those, who take this Mark, will suffer a worse hell on earth and below."*

Later, at Adoration, I could see several people without their heads and one of them wore a Roman collar of a priest. Jesus said: *"My people, I have not given you many details of the torture or means by which some of My faithful will be martyred. This is one of the more graphic descriptions that I have shown you of decapitated bodies. You remember very well how St. John the Baptist was killed, and you have read the Scriptures about those in the future who will be beheaded instead of taking the Mark of the Beast (Rev 20:4). These evil people, who will try to help contain the people for the Antichrist, will use any method to threaten people to worship the Antichrist. By making public displays of cruel killing of their opposition, they will try to force the people by fear to take the chip in the hand or forehead. I am telling you, My faithful, it is better to suffer a cruel death for My Name's sake, than to give in to the Antichrist and lose your soul. I will help you to withstand any pain that you may have to suffer in the tribulation. Fear not the one who can only kill the body, but fear the one who can bring your soul to eternal hell fire. I love you, My people, and I will be at your side to protect your soul. Call on My help, because you will not come to heaven without Me. Pray continually for your spiritual strength in this coming trial."*

Saturday, June 19, 1999:

After Communion, I could see a large circular stone covering a tomb. It rolled away by itself and Jesus rose in His glorified Body. Jesus said: *"My people, you are still on the earth dealing with the troubles of life each day. I have come to the earth to release you from your sins, but you must have faith in Me to be healed. It is in Confession that I forgive you your sins and it was by My death on the cross that I have redeemed you. So seek Me first as in the*

Gospel and I will provide all that you will need in this life. You are still in a state of being perfected, so do not be saddened that you are incomplete. Look forward to the one day I will resurrect your body and soul as radiant as My glorified body."

Later, at Nocturnal Adoration, I could see a face looking up to heaven. Then visions of my past life were refreshed with some old family pictures. Jesus said: *"My people, always keep your focus on Me and you will never be disappointed. There are times when you view old pictures, that you start to see how your spiritual life has progressed over the years. These moments of pondering what you have done in your life, help to keep you focused on your purpose here. Those, who are trying to please Me in their prayers and good deeds, are continually growing in their faith. Those, who are not prepared, will have a sudden shock of reality when they are faced with My Warning. For some, the Warning will be a wake-up call and may be a mercy to save their souls. Still others will refuse Me and accept the broad road to hell. Everyone has to decide what is more important — love of themselves or love of Me and their neighbors. When you give your will over to Me out of love, your soul will be satisfied in My peace. Follow Me by giving good example to those around you."*

Sunday, June 20, 1999: (Father's Day)

After Communion, I could see a large cave and God the Father said: *"I AM watches over all of My children more than your own fathers. During the coming tribulation your Heavenly Father will be waiting to provide you food and shelter. As I provided My people manna, you also will have a heavenly manna, if you have faith in My Son and ask Him. I am showing you this cave as a shelter that I could provide for you, if you lived near some hills or mountains. You will need protection from the Antichrist and the demons. I will call on your angels to guide you to a safe refuge. You will be tested for a brief time, but have trust and faith in My Fatherly love."*

Monday, June 21, 1999:

After Communion, I could look down on a gold judgment seat that was up high from the floor. Jesus said: *"My people, do not seek to judge others, because it is not your place to judge, but My own. I told you he, that lives by the sword, will die by the sword. In the same way the measure you use to judge others could be used to judge you. You would rather be judged by My mercy than by your own cruel justice. I also have told you many times to give good example and not to be a hypocrite in the way you behave. If you cannot abide by your own advice to others, then do not force on others' shoulders a burden that you cannot bear. Put your faith into your daily actions and live by My Commandments and your salvation will be assured."*

Later, at Adoration, I could see a large tank with its gun aimed down directly at me. Jesus said: *"My dear son, I am showing you this sign of a tank taking aim at you to emphasize the battle of good and evil that is going on in front of you. I have given you many public messages to prepare the people for the coming tribulation and to bring souls back to Confession before it is too late.... These are the End Times and there will be false prophets among the true ones. I ask everyone to read their Scriptures daily for discernment, and pray your three Rosaries so you can remain faithful to My Word. You will be tested dearly as the price of souls is why this battle of good and evil will become intense. Satan is doing everything in his power to lead souls away from Me with even miracles of deception. Keep your focus on your worship of Me only and pray for My help in everything you do to insure following My Will. Remember not to defend yourself, but always love and pray for everyone, even your persecutors."*

Tuesday, June 22, 1999: (St. John Fisher, St. Thomas More)

After Communion, I could see a surveillance camera. Jesus said: *"My people, for many years you have enjoyed your freedoms and rights. For many, these rights are now being compromised in the name of control of the thieves who use drugs and guns. Your technology is being used to control your everyday life. It is not uncommon to see cameras at banks, the workplace, stores, traffic lights, and the borders. These are all intrusions on your privacy and they are a means to follow all of your citizens. As the One World people tighten their controls on you, there will be a religious persecution to force people to only worship the Anti-*

christ. The martyrs of today's feast day had to stand up to the edicts of the king. Soon you will have to obey the edicts of the New World government which will put your life in jeopardy to believe in Me. When you will be tested by the authorities, are you going to be able to stand by My Name, even if it may mean being

martyred? On your own you would have difficulties, but with My help and that of the Holy Spirit, you will be given the endurance to even bear this challenge of martyrdom from the Antichrist."

Later, at Adoration, I could see some wheels moving of an amusement park. Jesus said: *"My people, you are not here on earth only to be amused and entertained. Every creature is made for My greater glory and as the angels, you are to know, love and serve Me. You are unique creatures of body and soul that are made in My image and you have free will to love Me or reject Me. Every life has been given a plan that only you are given to accomplish. I have given you My ways through My Ten Commandments. You are always in conflict between My ways and your ways. Life has many joys and sorrows that you will face every day. Each day has troubles of its own, so do not worry about tomorrow. You are tested in earning your living at work and dedicating your life to a vocation of single life, married life, or the religious life. You are always striving in faith to perfect yourself as you make yourself ready for your judgment. It is how you loved Me and loved your neighbor that you will be judged. You have My graces in My sacraments and My blessings that will lead you on your path to Heaven. During your life, I ask you to bear your cross of whatever you will encounter. Those, who refuse to follow Me and carry My cross, will see even more difficulties without My peace. Those, who love Me and do everything to please Me, will have a special joy in their hearts even on earth. Even though you will have trials to face, when you face them with My help, all will seem beautiful in your eyes. Your life here is one preparation for the day I will greet you in Heaven."*

Wednesday, June 23, 1999:

After Communion, I could see a podium with a lectionary opened. Jesus said: *"My people, as you look on this podium and read My Words, I am asking you to place My Gospel in your heart, so you can live your faith. It is one thing to hear My Words. It is another to believe in them. In today's reading it talks of a warning about false prophets and that you would recognize them in their bad fruits. This is not just a characteristic of false prophets. It is a lesson for everyone to understand, that you are what you do in your actions. You will be known by your actions both by Me and those observing your behavior. It is not enough to say 'Lord, Lord' in order to gain Heaven. You must live your faith daily in what you do. In order to prove that you are My disciples, you must abide by My Commandments and show your love for Me and your love for your neighbor. In giving witness that you are a Christian, you will be tested and judged on your actions. Your good example can be an inspiration to others to convert their lives to following Me. In all of this battle of good and evil, it all comes down to saving souls as being the most important thing you could do for Me. So watch your actions, because many people are watching to see if you are a hypocrite in what you believe. If you really believe in Me, your deeds and fruits should show it. Then at the judgment, your deeds will vouch for your entry into heaven."*

Later, at Adoration, I could see a top to a mosque and an Arab man wearing a white headpiece. Jesus said: *"My people, do not take much relief in the ending of your bombing campaign. The evil Serb leaders have killed and pillaged Kosovo even despite your bombing. Now you will have more troops tied down in peacekeeping. Your wars are not over. Many of the Arab nations are still engaged in terrorist activities and challenging you in Iraq and elsewhere. The day of Armageddon is building when the NATO countries will be defending Israel against the Arabs, Russia and China. NATO is becoming more of a force to back the European Union as the basis for a New World order. It will not be long when the Antichrist will come as a man of peace trying to settle the chaos that will come from wars and your computer problems. Pray continually for peace and that weapons of mass destruction are not used. Satan's time is short and he is trying to coerce as many into wars as he can. Satan is out to destroy man and he will join with the Antichrist ... to gain control over the world. Evil's reign will be brief, when I will come again in triumph to dash these evil spirits and evil people from the earth down into Hell. My faithful need to have hope and faith in Me, because My victory is soon and assured. I have been in control of all the powers that be and I have allowed this trial to test your faith in Me. So pray for spiritual strength in My grace and rejoice for the day you will see your reward in paradise."*

Thursday, June 24, 1999: (The birth of St. John the Baptist)

After Communion, I could see some Roman pillars of buildings. Jesus said: *"My people, St. John the Baptist was the last of those who proclaimed My First Coming. He was a pillar of strength in faith and his inspirations for conversion and repentance are still needed today. In those days of My First Coming there was a strong dominance by a Roman secular army. There are parallels with My Second Coming as well. My blessed mother Mary has been the new Eve preparing the way for My glorious triumph. Mary has foretold to you in messages and apparitions the same preparation of prayer and repentance. She has reached out in motherly love for her children, to bring you back to your knees in prayer and fasting.... You will have to be pillars of faith also through My help, My mother and your angels. There are many prophets even in your own day that are heralding My coming. Their same message is one of both spiritual and physical preparation. You are facing an evil battle, but take heart and have no fear, because I will remove all evil from the earth and My peace and love will reign supreme."*

Later, at the prayer group, I could see the tops of some buildings decorated with pagan gods and goddesses. Jesus said: *"My people, in past days man worshiped gods of the earth and mythical gods and goddesses. Even some of these pagan gods were gods of the underworld. Your people are again taking up these pagan rituals to demonic spirits. There are many evil covens worshiping the devil. The latest wickens or white witches, being allowed in the army, are a means to show you that they exist. Do not be misled by such pagan worship. I am the only God of the universe worthy of your praise of My glory."*

I could see various kingdoms spread as far as the eye could see. Jesus said: *"My people, there are many nations and many leaders struggling to control them. Do not be so concerned with power and lording it over others. It is better for you to submit yourself to someone whom you have to make an accounting. If you have difficulties in being under someone's control in your earthly life, how will you be able to submit your will to following My Will in your spiritual life? So seek to follow Me in everything and I will reward your faithfulness."*

I could see lanterns of oil lamps and candles being used. Jesus said: *"My people, during your power outages, those, who were prepared, had candles and lanterns for light. As the wise virgins had extra oil for their lamps, you also should be prepared for electricity outages in the event of failures in your power plants. A light sustained in the darkness allows you to see clearly. I am the Light of the world that blots out the darkness of your sins with My victory over death. Remain faithful to Me and you will see spiritually clear as well."*

I could see some very beautiful castles and some elegant homes. Jesus said: *"My people, do not spend all of your lives chasing after rich homes and fancy cars. There is more to life than desiring the things of this world. Once you acquire your dreams, there is a big letdown because it will not satisfy your souls. Only My peace can give rest to your souls. That is why eternal riches in Heaven are much more desirable, for they will not fade away, but they will be your witness to My love. Seek Me first and I will grace you with all that you will need."*

I could look down on a large table with many leaders of your world's finances coming together in a meeting. Jesus said: *"My people, your evil financial masters of the One World government are planning your demise in how they will confiscate your money and your possessions. These leaders want more than money. They want to have complete control all over the earth. They will soon use your wars and computer problems to create a crisis for which only they will have the answers. They will be preparing the way for the Mark of the Beast to be the only source of buying and selling. It is the Antichrist who will come and answer your problems under the guise of peace. Rely only on My help and you will survive this evil."*

I could see some major crevasses in the earth caused by some huge earthquakes. Jesus said: *"My people, there will be a gradual increase in the frequency of your major earthquakes and an increase in their intensity. These deep crevasses will make dramatic changes in the appearance of the earth. Many lives will be threatened by these events. Do not lose heart, for these things must come to pass as the Bible has foretold. They are one of the many signs of the End Times, but also an indication of My Second Coming."*

I could see some men bringing Jesus' Body to be placed in the tomb. Jesus said: *"My people, several times I told My apostles that I would be crucified by My own people and that I would rise again on the third day. My disciples were still not enlightened by the Holy Spirit to understand what rising from the dead meant. It was explained to St. Peter, St. John and St. James about My Glorified Body at My Transfiguration. But it was not until I appeared to My apostles that they fully believed in My promise. This is your perfected body that you will have after your resurrection. Rejoice in My promise for your eternal salvation, and obey My Commandments in following Me. This life in the eternal now is your goal for your soul to share in My everlasting peace. This is your prize and everything that you should be living for in this life. Everything else in this life falls short of My glory in Heaven. Focus your life on pleasing Me and you will find rest for your soul."*

Friday, June 25, 1999:

At St. Joseph's Adoration, Prince Albert, Saskatchewan, Canada, I could see a large building in the open that housed the government of Canada and it immediately fell completely to the ground. Jesus said: *"My people, a time is coming when all of the governments of the world will crumble and fall into the hands of the Antichrist. Many do not want to believe that this can happen, but this is how it is written in the Bible. Once the Antichrist has assumed power, he will assign ten leaders as his puppets to help him control the whole world. He will set up a Mark of his image to be worshiped and he will force everyone to buy and sell using his Mark that will be placed in the right hand or forehead. The monied people of the New World Order will control this new means of exchange through the central banks all over the world. There will be a network of satellites to control all of this buying and selling. My faithful will refuse to accept this authority in their lives. There will be a schism in My church that will force My true believers to go underground away from the evil influences of ... the Antichrist. Refuse this evil money system where these chips will control those who take these chips in their bodies. I will provide for your protection, your food and your shelter. Just have faith in Me and you will have nothing to fear."*

Saturday, June 26, 1999:

At Our Lady of Czestochowa, Prince Albert, Saskatchewan, Canada, after Communion, I could see Jesus in Heaven and then a tomb being opened. Jesus said: *"My people, I am calling everyone of My faithful to be with Me in Heaven. As My apostles watched Me ascending into Heaven, they were saddened by My leaving, but they were awestruck by the magnificence of Heaven. My angels promised them that I would return to earth on clouds of majesty in My triumph. So do not be fearful of what lies ahead in your next life. Everything you do on earth should be directed to follow Me in preparation for your coming to Heaven. By My help and your endurance, you will one day see Me in all of My glory. This should be the main focus of your life here on earth that you should desire Heaven over everything on earth. When you receive Me in Holy Communion, I am giving you just a taste of My love and peace that will be forever yours. You will struggle for a while on earth, but your efforts will not be in vain. For all those, who give Me praise and are obedient to all of My requests, they will one day enjoy seeing Me as I am in My beatific vision. This joy in My presence will go beyond all of your comprehension of My love. You will experience Me so completely that words will not express the way you will be a part of My Divine Presence. So come, My children, and do not tarry, but accept Me wholly into your life without any reservations."*

Sunday, June 27, 1999:

At Assumption Church, Edmonton, Alberta, Canada, after Communion, I could see Our Lord laying in the tomb and then He came alive again in glory. Jesus said: *"My people, death has no hold on Me. I have come as a man so that I may endure all of your pains and disappointments. I love all of you so much that I wished to show My love for you through My sufferings. It was by My own free will that I gave up My life so that your sins may be forgiven and that you would have new life in the Spirit. Do not see My death as one event that is over, because you relive that experience at the unbloody sacrifice of every Mass. My blood washes out your sins. Death has been a weakness of your bodies passed on from the effects of original sin. With My opening of the Gates of*

Heaven for all mankind, one day My faithful will rise again to enjoy the full life I intended for every soul in Heaven. At My triumph you will soon be blessed with glorified bodies with your souls. Death's bonds will be broken from all of you. Rejoice, My people, as you look forward to sharing in the glory of your Lord."

Later, at St. Andrew's Church, Edmonton, Alberta, Canada, I could see a teacher and a large pool with younger children swimming. Jesus said: *"My people, each teacher becomes involved with knowing the lives of their students. That teacher works faithfully on each lesson to teach their course of study and helps the students to understand and be proficient in their work. I am your greatest teacher and I want to save each soul that I have created. I want to be a part of each life so I can help you in your daily troubles. My lessons for you are found in My Gospels, so you can learn to imitate My life of love. I have shown My interest in saving your souls by My death on the cross. Just as a student must study, so you too must read My Word so you will know how to follow My Commandments. Again, each student is tested at the end to see if they can pass the course. You will be tested also at your judgment as to whether you are worthy of passing into Heaven. Loving Me is more than just having a book knowledge of the faith. It takes a life long struggle to restrain the body and focus all of your efforts to following My ways. But those, who fight the battle of good and evil and run the course for My sake, will have a heavenly reward beyond their comprehension."*

Monday, June 28, 1999:

At St. Andrew's Church, Edmonton, Alberta, Canada, after Communion, I could see a well for water and a Mass was said at that place. Jesus said: *"My people, in the old days people had to come to the well for their daily water needs. But I call you to My living water and My heavenly bread of the Mass. Just as you cannot survive without water, so also your soul cannot survive without My Presence in your life. When I call on you to follow Me, it is not just a momentary commitment, but a lifelong commitment to obey My laws. As the water refreshes your body, so receiving Me in Holy Communion refreshes your soul. I have told you that man does not live by bread alone, but by the Word of*

My Heavenly Father. You all are called to follow Me in your earthly lives so you can prepare to be with Me in your next life in Heaven. Hold firm in your desire to follow Me and never lose that fervor of your first love of Me in your conversion. Continue your daily prayers so you can communicate your love to Me."

Tuesday, June 29, 1999: (Sts. Peter & Paul)

At Holy Family Church, Saskatoon, Saskatchewan, Canada, after Communion, I could see an old building where an underground Mass was being said. Jesus said: *"My people, in the days of St. Paul and St. Peter there were many who did not want to change the old religious teachings. I came to fulfill the law and to die for your sins. That is why I gave a new Commandment to love God and your neighbor as yourselves. It was My teachings of forgiving everyone and enduring insults that made people uncomfortable with My way of love. Because My Word was not comfortable and a threat to their way of living, some persecuted My apostles and My believers. It was an act of faith to recognize Me as the Messiah. But it is a blessing to be able to give your life up for My Name's sake. This is the same test that My faithful will have to endure during the coming tribulation. Do not be misled by either the Antichrist or any religious that will worship anyone else but Me. There will come a day when you will need to have underground Masses, where a priest can be found. You will even have to refuse the Mark of the Beast and trust that I will provide for you. The evil people will even threaten to kill you for believing in My Name and not worshiping the image of the beast. Pray for My help and I will protect your souls from any evil influence."*

Wednesday, June 30, 1999:

At Adoration, I could see a narrow hall of stone and there was a sense of the traditional early Christian faith. Jesus said: *"My people, in the early days of Christianity there was much persecution of My followers. Many of them had to be in hiding to keep from being killed by their persecutors. They walked through catacombs, but they had no fear because of their faith in Me. I am showing you these walls of stone because a time of trial is coming again when you will see religious persecution. My faithful today are only mildly scorned by some for your belief in My Name.*

This persecution will come to the point where these evil men will seek to kill you for believing in Me. My faithful remnant I will protect through My help and that of My angels. Call on Me at that time, for without Me, you will not save your souls. Even though you may be tested as My early martyrs, do not be afraid, for My power is greater than any power of Satan or the Antichrist. You will not be tested beyond My grace to endure your trials. So have peace in these events, because I will soon be coming in triumph to restore My glory in the New Jerusalem....

Prepare for the Great Tribulation and the Era of Peace

Index

Prepare for the Great Tribulation and the Era of Peace

Church not destroyed
    promise of Jesus (Jesus) — 4/3/99
Churches
    burned and desecrated (Jesus) — 6/7/99
comet of chastisement
    to consume lost sinners (Jesus) — 5/3/99
    triumph over evil (Jesus) — 5/6/99
comfort threatened
    forgiveness,taking insults (Jesus) — 6/29/99
communication
    in marriage, prayers (Jesus) — 6/2/99
complaining
    put on a happy face (Jesus) — 5/26/99
computer failures
    return to simple life (Jesus) — 6/10/99
computers
    puffed up in technology (Jesus) — 6/1/99
    to stop working (Jesus) — 6/17/99
conference
    workers for Father's honor (God the Father) 4/17/99
Confession
    a haven for sinners (Jesus) — 5/31/99
    always be prepared (Jesus) — 6/4/99
    brings closer to perfection (Jesus) — 5/27/99
    cleanses our sins (Jesus) — 6/13/99
    life raft from sins (Jesus) — 4/15/99
    sins forgiven (Jesus) — 6/19/99
    state of sanctifying grace (Jesus) — 5/17/99
Confession needed
    remove darkness of soul (Jesus) — 4/10/99
conflict in soul
    between our ways & God (Jesus) — 6/22/99
contrite heart
    finds rest in Jesus (Jesus) — 4/19/99
cornerstone rejected
    by scribes & pharisees (Jesus) — 4/15/99
cross of Calvary
    everyone has to carry one (Jesus) — 5/2/99
cross of life
    all carry it to Calvary (Jesus) — 4/5/99
Cross, daily
    must be suffered (Jesus) — 4/24/99
crucifix
    sign of our redemption (Jesus) — 5/6/99

crucifix on altar
    remember Jesus' death (Jesus) — 4/8/99
crucifixes with corpus
    need in churches, homes (Jesus) — 5/1/99
death
    always be prepared for (Jesus) — 5/17/99
    has no hold on Jesus (Jesus) — 6/27/99
death culture
    seeking rights to kill (Jesus) — 4/22/99
despair of the poor
    dispel with love (Jesus) — 4/14/99
detention centers
    evil men controlling people (Jesus) — 4/29/99
    for those refusing mark (Jesus) — 4/7/99
Divine Will
    be good examples (Jesus) — 5/10/99
    give up pride,selfishness (Jesus) — 5/19/99
DNA manipulated
    man exploiting for profit (Jesus) — 4/27/99
door of your heart
    hospitality to Jesus (Jesus) — 4/19/99
dress at Mass
    should be respectful (Jesus) — 6/8/99
earthquakes
    to change face of earth (Jesus) — 6/24/99
Easter celebration
    triumph of Jesus (Jesus) — 4/3/99
Era of Peace
    faithful raised up (Jesus) — 6/15/99
    paradise recreated (Jesus) — 6/17/99
    well worth the wait (Jesus) — 6/10/99
eternal destiny
    worth more than long life (Jesus) — 4/20/99
Eucharist
    most important gift (Jesus) — 4/7/99
    spiritual bread,food of soul (Jesus) — 4/22/99
Exodus
    repeated today (Jesus) — 6/10/99
    will leave in haste (Jesus) — 6/18/99
Exodus manna
    similar miracles (Jesus) — 4/23/99
eyes of faith
    to know love of God,other (Jesus) — 5/4/99
faith & right reason
    breastplate & helmet (Jesus) — 4/27/99

Prepare for the Great Tribulation and the Era of Peace

More Messages

If you would like to take advantage of more precious words from Jesus and Mary and apply them to your lives, read the first three volumes of messages and visions given to us through John's special gift. Each book contains a full year of daily messages and visions. As Jesus and Mary said in volume IV:

> *Listen to My words of warning, and you will be ready to share in the beauty of the Second Coming.* Jesus 7/4/96
> *I will work miracles of conversion on those who read these books with an open mind.* Jesus 9/5/96

Prepare for the Great Tribulation and the Era of Peace

Volume I - *July 1993 to June 1994,* ISBN# 1-882972-69-4, 256pp.	$7.95
Volume II - *July 1994 to June 1995,* ISBN# 1-882972-72-4, 352pp.	$8.95
Volume III - *July 1995 to July 10, 1996,* ISBN# 1-882972-77-5, 384pp.	$8.95
Volume IV - *July 11, 1996 to Sept. 30, 1996,* ISBN# 1-882972-91-0, 104pp.	$3.95
Volume V - *Oct. 1, 1996 to Dec. 31, 1996,* ISBN# 1-882972-97-X, 120pp.	$3.95
Volume VI - *Jan. 1, 1997 to Mar. 31, 1997,* ISBN# 1-57918-002-7, 112pp.	$3.95
Volume VII - *April 1, 1997 to June 30, 1997,* ISBN# 1-57918-010-8, 112pp.	$3.95
Volume VIII - *July 1, 1997 to Sept. 30, 1997,* ISBN# 1-57918-053-1, 128pp.	$3.95
Volume IX - *Oct. 1, 1997 to Dec. 31, 1997,* ISBN# 1-57918-066-3, 168pp.	$3.95
Volume X - *Jan. 1, 1998 to Mar. 31, 1998,* ISBN# 1-57918-073-6, 116pp.	$3.95
Volume XI - *Apr. 1, 1998 to June 30, 1998,* ISBN# 1-57918-096-5, 128pp.	$3.95
Volume XII - *July 1, 1998 to Sept. 30, 1998,* ISBN# 1-57918-105-8, 128pp.	$3.95
Volume XIII - *Oct. 1, 1998 to Dec. 31, 1998,* ISBN# 1-57918-113-9, 134pp.	$3.95
Volume XIV - *Jan. 1, 1999 to Mar. 31, 1999,* ISBN# 1-57918-115-5, 128pp.	$3.95

Other Great Titles From
QUEENSHIP PUBLISHING
From your local Catholic bookstore or direct from the Publisher

Trial, Tribulation and Triumph
Before, During and After Antichrist
Desmond Birch
ISBN# 1-882972-73-2 .... $19.50

The Amazing Secret of the Souls in Purgatory
An Interview with Maria Simma
Sr. Emmanuel of Medjugorje
ISBN# 1-57918-004-3 .... $4.95

After the Darkness
A Catholic Novel on the Coming of the Antichrist
and the End of the World
Rev. Joseph M. Esper
ISBN# 1-57918-048-5 .... $14.95

Mary's Three Gifts to Her Beloved Priests
A Deeper Understanding of Our Lady's Messages to Fr. Gobbi
Rev. Albert Shamon
ISBN# 1-57918-005-1 .... $2.95

The Final Warning
And a Defense Against Modernism
Paul A. Mihalik, Sr., Lt. Colonel USAF (Ret.)
ISBN# 1-57918-043-4 .... $4.95

A Light Shone in the Darkness
The Story of the Stigmatist and Mystic
Therese Neumann of Konnersreuth
Doreen Mary Rossman
ISBN# 1-57918-044-2 .... $12.95

Unabridged Christianity
Biblical Answers to Common Question
about the Roman Catholic Faith
Fr. Mario Romero
ISBN# 1-57918-056-6 .... $12.95

Catholic Pocket Evangelist
Biblical Outlines for Scripturaly-Based
Discussions of the Roman Catholic Faith.
Fr. Mario Romero
ISBN# 1-57918-057-4 .... $2.95